The Bible Our Textbook for Life

Mat 13:44 "Again, the kingdom of heaven is like unto treasure hid in a field; the which when a man hath found, he hideth, and for joy thereof goeth and selleth all that he hath, and buyeth that field." (King James Version, 2012, Matt. 13:44)

ISBN: 978-1-312-55692-8

Contents

Bibles Used

Introduction

I wanted to take this time to introduce myself and tell you a little bit about why I wrote it. My name is Robert Riddle Jr. and I am the Sr. pastor of a small none denominational church called Little Brooks Chapel. I have a bachelor in Biblical studies and have taken Bible classes from Grand Canyon University; I also have a certificate in the Life of Christ from Rhema Bible School and a certificate in Biblical counseling from Light University a branch of Trinity Bible University.

I live in a small town in Texas with my wife of 21 years and youngest daughter who is now 18 my oldest daughter lives in Waco and she is 20. I thank God that we all love Jesus and his word and are church goers. My wife and love to spend time together in the word and going church, we also love to watch movies and play games mostly card games.

I get into why I wrote this book a little later on in chapter one, but I thought this would be a good time to get a little deeper into why I wrote this book.

You might be thinking that I wrote this book to help learn how to study and yes that is true, but the reason is much deeper than that. Let me explain.

I have run into those in the cults many times in fact I even have formal debates with them from time to time and the main thing that I find common among them is that they have taken Bible verses out of context and the sad thing is they are getting people to fall for there lies because they do not know how to study the Bible for themselves. People hear someone that uses big words and sound like they know what they are talking about and the hook is set they are falling for the lie and joining false churches. I know because I was almost one of them.

One of the objections to learning how to interpret is that people will say that the Bible is not left up to any private interpretation according to 2 Peter 1:20. Well the fact is there right we cannot use our own interpretation when it comes to studying the Bible. However, we all interpret when we read we cannot help it, but we can learn how to do it rightly just like the Bible says in 2Ti 2:15 “Study to shew thyself approved unto God, a workman that needeth not to be ashamed, rightly dividing the word of truth.” (King James Version 2 Tim. 2:15)

Remember the Bible tells us Isa 28:10 “For precept must be upon precept, precept upon precept; line upon line, line upon line; here a little, and there a little” (King James Version Isa 28:10). The way I like to put it is like this, you can look at like a jigsaw puzzle there are millions of pieces and if you put them together they make a beautiful picture. However if you get the pieces wrong or try to make them fit together when they don’t you get something distorted. This is why we need to learn how to interpret the Bible so we get all the pieces put together right.

Yes we cannot interpret the Bible on our own that will lead us down a very bad path we do not want to be on however, the Bible will interpret itself and we have the Holy Spirit to teach us all things John 14:26 “But the Comforter, which is the Holy Ghost, whom the Father will send in my name, he shall teach you all things, and bring all things to your remembrance, whatsoever I have said unto you.” (King James Version John 14:26)

So with that said let’s learn how to study the Bible. Have fun and remember you can do it because the Bible says in Philippians 4:13 “I can do all things through Christ which strengtheneth me.” (King James Version Philippians 4:13)

Chapter One Why Study?

Why study the Bible? Well, why do we study anything? Don't we study anything so that we can learn? The answer is yes; if we want to be anything from a doctor to a welder, to a mechanic to a teacher or anything else, we have to study.

You might be saying at this point, but I am not going to be a preacher or a Sunday school teacher or a missionary. Ok, that may be true for now however, we do not know what tomorrow may bring; you might wake up and hear the call to ministry and to be honest we are all in the ministry, we are all called to witness to people, We will be looking at this a little later on. However, the thing that I would like to stress here is we are teaching people every day by how we live or do not live the Word. What I mean here is quite simple, we live what we learn from the Word and others see it or they do not see it. I can always tell when my congregation really heard a message because I see them doing it. But I ask how are we going to know how to live if we do not study the Bible?

If we don't study, we don't learn ; it's that simple and if we don't learn, how can we do it? The same is true with our Christian walk with the lord, if we want to be the best Christian we can be then we need to take the time to study the Bible.

Why study the Bible? Well, I heard a great acronym and I have no idea where it came from, but I love it and it goes like this:

- B = Basic
- I= instructions
- B = Before
- L= Leaving
- E = Earth

I love this acronym because it really is the truth about what the Bible is. The Bible gives us instructions on how to live our life to the fullest so that we can be all that we can for

God, to grow spiritually and to be the witnesses that we are supposed to be for God.

I know some of you might be asking; can't I just read the Bible, after all I am still getting into the Bible? The answer is no, you can't just read the Bible; however, if you are doing that I applaud you because most Christians don't even do that. Most people leave their Bible laying around and collecting dust which reminds me of a bluegrass song by Hank Williams Sr., Dust on the Bible. The first verse goes like this:

> I went into a home one day just to see some friends of mine Of all their books and magazines, not a Bible could I find I asked them for the Bible when they brought it, what a shame For the dust was covered o'er it, not a fingerprint was plain
>
> Chorus
>
> Dust on the Bible, dust on the Holy Word The words of all the prophets and the sayings of our Lord Of all the other books you'll find, there's none salvation holds Get the dust off the Bible and redeem your poor soul (metrolyrics.com, n.d., Dust on the Bible Lyrics, Hank Williams Sr. Para. 1-2)

I think this is so true when it comes to most Christians or they put it out to look good for when the preacher comes over. So, if you are reading the Bible good for you; at least you are doing more than most, but now take it a step further; dig into it and get the vast amount of treasure that is in there.

We also need to remember that the Bible is not a novel or a good book as some are prone to calling it. The Bible is more than good stories, I admit there are some really cool stories in the Bible like Jonah and the great fish, Samson and Delilah and many more however, but if we just read them we are not getting the real meaning out of them. We need to dig in and get out all that we can.

I like this Bible verse a lot: Prov. 2:1-11 that says:

> "My son, if thou wilt receive my words, and hide my commandments with thee; So that thou incline thine ear unto wisdom, *and* apply thine heart to understanding; Yea, if thou criest after knowledge, *and* liftest up thy

voice for understanding; If thou seekest her as silver, and searchest for her as *for* hid treasures; Then shalt thou understand the fear of the LORD, and find the knowledge of God. For the LORD giveth wisdom: out of his mouth *cometh* knowledge and understanding. He layeth up sound wisdom for the righteous: *he is* a buckler to them that walk uprightly. He keepeth the paths of judgment, and preserveth the way of his saints. Then shalt thou understand righteousness, and judgment, and equity; *yea,* every good path. When wisdom entereth into thine heart, and knowledge is pleasant unto thy soul; Discretion shall preserve thee, understanding shall keep thee:" (King James Version, 2012, Prov. 2:1-11)

These Bible verses are so true, but I think the New Century Version puts it in a way that makes it even more clear the value of studying the Bible.

"My child, listen to what I say and remember what I command you. Listen carefully to wisdom; set your mind on understanding. Cry out for wisdom, and beg for understanding. Search for it like silver, and hunt for it like hidden treasure. Then you will understand respect for the LORD, and you will find that you know God. Only the LORD gives wisdom; he gives knowledge and understanding. He stores up wisdom for those who are honest. Like a shield he protects the innocent. He makes sure that justice is done, and he protects those who are loyal to him. Then you will understand what is honest and fair and what is the good and right thing to do. Wisdom will come into your mind, and knowledge will be pleasing to you. Good sense will protect you; understanding will guard you." (New Century Version, 2005, Prov. 2:1-11)

Think about the Bible this way, the Bible is a textbook; I mean if you think about it, that is what we would study from when we were in school is our are textbooks. Now the Bible tells us clearly in 2 Tim. 2:15 "Study to shew thyself approved unto God, a workman that needeth not to be ashamed, rightly dividing the word of truth." (King James

Version, 2012, Prov. 2:1-11) We will look at this verse a little later on. However, it says study the word making it our text book for life.

Another reason we need to be studying our Bible is because we do not want to give into seducing sprits and doctrines of devils. Look at what the Bible says in 1 Tim. 4:1: "Now the Spirit speaketh expressly, that in the latter times some shall depart from the faith, giving heed to seducing spirits, and doctrines of devils" (King James Version, 2012, 1 Tim. 4:1) Again, let's look at this from the New Century Version it says: "Now the Holy Spirit clearly says that in the later times some people will stop believing the faith. They will follow spirits that lie and teachings of demons." (New Century Version, 2005, 1 Tim. 4:1)

We can see here clearly that Paul is warning us in the last days (days that we are living in now) that some shall depart from the faith by two things: seducing spirits and doctrines of the devil or false doctrines. Now the word doctrine means: "*did-as-kal-ee'-ah* From G1320; *instruction* (the function or the information): - doctrine, learning, teaching." (Meyers, E-Sword (Version 10.1 Computer Software 2012, Strong's dictionary). So how do we find the teachings or the doctrines of the Bible? You got it, from studying the Bible. My friends, I don't want you to be one of them that falls to seducing spirits and doctrines of devils.

Let's face it, there are so many false teachers out there and false churches so we need to know the truth so we don't fall prey and get off into left field. Sad to say, Christians are falling for them because to tell you the truth, they don't know the true doctrines. I have seen it time and time again where good Christians have fallen for the lies of the devil, Evolution is a good example of that. Most Christians will say yea God created everything, but it took millions of years or if you ask them how long ago did dinosaurs live? They say millions of years ago. This is a lie that they have fallen into because of ignorance.

Now, this would be a good place to go back to what I said earlier about 2 Tim. 2:15 "Study to shew you approved unto God, a workman that needeth not to be ashamed, rightly dividing the word of truth." (King James Version, 2012, Prov. 2:1-11) and the Bible being our textbook. Clearly this verse tells us why we need to study and that is "to be a workman". How are we going to know what to do if we don't study the Bible? Simply put, we won't, as I have said before; the Bible is our Basic instructions before leaving earth.

We also need to understand that 2 Tim. 2:15 is not a suggestion; it's a commandment. When we look at this verse it is not saying if you feel like it or it might be good for you to study, if you can fit it into your planner; no, Paul is clearly giving us a direct command: STUDY, end of story. Now, because it is a commandment; if we do not do it, then we are in sin. Look at this verse: James 4:17 "Therefore to him that knoweth to do good, and doeth *it* not, to him it is sin." " (King James Version, 2012, James. 4:17)

> The Bible gives us the measuring stick by which we can distinguish truth from error. It tells us what God is like. To have a wrong impression of God is to worship an idol or false god. We are worshiping something that He is not. (Why read/study the Bible, 2011, par. 4)

Now Jesus said in John 14:15 "If ye love me, keep my commandments." (King James Version, 2012, John 14:15) Now you can say that the commandment to study is from Paul, not Jesus, however, the whole Bible is inspired by the Holy Spirit: 2 Timothy 3:16: "All scripture is given by inspiration of God, and is profitable for doctrine, for reproof, for correction, for instruction in righteousness." (King James Version, 2012, 2 Tim. 3:16) Now think about this the Bible says that God breathed into Adam the breath of life and man became a living soul Gen. 2:7 now the word inspiration means to "divinely breathed in" (Meyers, 2012, E-Sword, Version 10.1 Computer Software, Retrieved October 18, 2012, 2012) with that said we can honestly say that God wrote the whole Bible. Also think about this because it was divinely breathed in the men that penned the Bible the Bible is the living word.

I think that if Christians were really honest with themselves, God and others, they would have to say they are ashamed because they have not been good workmen. They do not know really what the Bible teaches about things beyond salvation and most cannot even teach on salvation or how to get saved because they have not taken the time to study it. I remember a time when my wife and I moved to a new town and we were looking for a church to attend, I stopped at some that were non denominational churches and when I asked the people what their statement of faith was, they were like "I don't know." or "You have to ask our pastor." I was like, what the heck is going on here; people do not even know what they believe? I was blown away and saddened.

Another thing is, if we are not seeing our prayers answered like we would like, then we need to look at this verse: John 9:31 "Now we know that God heareth not sinners: but if any man be a worshipper of God, and doeth his will, him he heareth" (King James Version, 2012, John 9:31). Here we see that God does not hear sinners and I hate to break it to you, but if you commit a sin, that makes you a sinner, right? Of course it does and as we saw, not studying is a sin. Not only that, but it goes on to say the one that does His (God's) will is the one He hears. Well, studying the Bible is God's will otherwise the Bible would not say "Study".

Now please do not get me wrong here, I do not want to make anyone feel condemned, but at the same time, I am not going to sugar coat the Bible or pat people on the head and tell them everything is alright when it's not.

One of the other reasons we need to study is like I said earlier, there are many false teachers and churches out there. So we need to be ready with truth, look at what the Bible tells us in 1 Pet. 3:15: "But sanctify the Lord God in your hearts: and *be* ready always to *give* an answer to every man that asketh you a reason of the hope that is in you with meekness and fear:" (King James Version, 2012, 1 Pet. 3:15) "But respect Christ as the holy Lord in your hearts. Always be ready to answer everyone who asks you to explain about the hope you have" (New Century Version, 2005, 1 Pet. 3:15) and look at: "But in your hearts set Christ apart as holy [and acknowledge Him] as Lord. Always be ready to give a logical defense to anyone who asks you to account for the hope that is in you, but do it courteously and respectfully." (Amplified Bible, 1987, I Pet. 3:15)

Now the only way we can give answers to people's questions or come against false teachings is by knowing what the Bible really teaches and the only way we can know is to study.

On a personal note, I can say with all honesty that getting deep into the word of God and learning how to study the right way has not only brought me closer to God, but has helped me to be a better person in general (So my wife tells me LOL)

I can really relate however, to Prov. 2 when it uses the phrase "hidden treasure." I can remember when I first started digging into the Word; I was like a kid in a candy shop that was told he could have all he wanted. I ate it up and as fast as I could and I learned so many cool things. Every time God showed me something new, I would run and tell my wife, many times I woke her up at 2 or 3 in the morning saying, "Honey, look at the gold nugget God just gave me". That is what it was for me, gold nuggets; and not only was it valuable, but it was precious to me. People would laugh at me because I would get so excited, I had to tell anyone that would listen no matter where I was, and (By the way, I am still the same way lol). I just cannot keep it in, I have to tell someone or I will blow up, I can relate to Jeremiah when he said "the word of the Lord was like a fire shut up in his bones."

> Studying the Bible can be compared to mining for gold. If we make little effort and merely "sift through the pebbles in a stream," we will only find a little gold dust. But the more we make an effort to really dig into it, the more reward we will gain for our effort. (Why read/study the Bible, 2011, para. 7)

Another reason we need to study the Word is it helps us to see what sin does to a person and we can learn from studying the mistakes that they, in the Bible, made. It is a whole lot easier on us if we learn from them instead of learning from experience. For example, we can learn from Moses the great prophet of God that sin can stop us from getting the good things that God has for us. Remember, because of his sin he was only allowed to see the Promised Land, he could not enter it and you can see that in Numbers chapter 20.

Not only do we learn about the effects of sin in our lives, but we can also see our faith grow in God by studying what God has done for others. We learn that God wants us to have good things and He gives them to us. All you have to do is look at the promises that God gave us and we can see Him keep those promises in the lives of the people in the Bible. For example, look at this promise in Exo. 14:14: "The LORD shall fight for you, and ye shall hold your peace." Now we take that to the story of David and Goliath, David ,in 1 Sam. 17, it recalls the times when God protected him and gave him strength to overcome the wild beast; this gave David peace when he walked out onto that battlefield and what happened? God won the battle. Yes, David was the one with the stone, but it was God that made the stone do its job. Or we can look at Moses again when he led the chosen people out of Egypt, God parted the waters, but when the army was about to get to them, the waters collapsed and killed them all. I can go on and on with this as it gets me excited. However, I might save that for another book.

I think we need to go back to the Bible verse 1 Peter 3:15: "But sanctify the Lord God in your hearts: and *be* ready always to *give* an answer to every man that asketh you a reason of the hope that is in you with meekness and fear." (King James Version, 2012, 1 Pet. 3:15) I believe this can also refer to teaching, be ready to teach those that ask you for a reason of the hope that is in you.

Now how are you going to teach that which you don't know? You can't, it is that simple, you can't. Think about it this way; if I go and apply for a teaching position at any school, high school or college to teach for example: teach people how to be a heart specialist and I have never studied it myself; for starters what do you think the school will say to me? Boy you're nuts, but even if they did hire me, how am I going to teach them? Would you want to put your life in the hands of one of my students? Umm, I don't think so. So how are we going to teach others the Bible, even the basics of the Bible, if we first did not study it ourselves?

I know what some of you are thinking "I am not called to teach or be a teacher." That may be; not everyone is called to the office of a teacher. However, we are still called to teach in one way or another. Look at this verse: Col. 3:16 "Let the word of Christ dwell in you richly in all wisdom; teaching and admonishing one another in psalms and hymns and spiritual songs, singing with grace in your hearts to the Lord." (King James Version, 2012, Col. 3:16) Now think about this: every time we sing, we are teaching. Look at the things we learned in songs from the world, most are not good, but when we sing songs to the Lord, what we are teaching others; for example: like the love God has for us in such songs as "Jesus loves Me" or we teach on the power of God in songs like "Power In The Blood," the list can go on and on here. The thing is, like it or not, we are teaching, especially the kids. (Makes us think what we are teaching our kids when we play songs like "I Got Friends in Low Places." Many times I have said and believe that the songs we sing are our sermons in themselves.

Teaching is More than sitting down in a classroom, we all learn from watching each other; even Jesus said in John 14:12: "Verily, verily, I say unto you, He that believeth on me, the works that I do shall he do also; and greater works than these shall he do; because I go unto my Father." (King James Version, 2012, John 14:12). Simply put, they learned what to do by watching Jesus do them.

Now look at this verse: 2Tim. 3:16 "All scripture *is* given by inspiration of God, and *is* profitable for doctrine, for reproof, for correction, for instruction in righteousness:" (King James Version, 2012, 2 Tim. 3:16) The word doctrine means "*did-as-kal-ee'-ah* From G1320; *instruction* (the function or the information): - doctrine, learning, teaching." (Meyers, E-Sword (Version 10.1 Computer Software) , 2012, Strong's dictionary) as we see it means teaching along with learning because as I have said so many times you cannot teach what you don't know.

You can see that Paul was talking to Timothy, but even if He was, then nothing in the Bible applies to us because the Bible was written to other people or groups of people. For example, Jesus was not talking to the church or to us today however, we still apply what He said to our lives. But, if we said He was not talking to us ,then we don't need to apply it to us, so then wouldn't we all still be lost and in our sin? Sure we would because Jesus was talking to a specific group of people.

Now look at this: Jesus said in Mat. 22:37 and 39 to love God with everything we have and to love our neighbor as ourselves right and we try to apply this to our lives, but why? Jesus was talking to a lawyer. The point I am trying to make here is just because the verse is not talking to us does not mean it does not apply to us.

I must stress this in finishing up this chapter : we do not study the Bible to merely get head knowledge (In fact if that is your only purpose for reading this book then put it away or give it to someone else.) . Head knowledge is good, don't get me wrong however, when it comes to the Bible, it is meant to be applied to our life. It is not to make us look good or smart so we can be prideful or to make people like us. "Otherwise, it is like swallowing food without chewing and then spitting it back out again—no nutritional value is gained by it." (Why read/study the Bible, 2011, para. 7)

Not only that, but we must remember what James told us in Jas. 1:22-25: "But be ye doers of the word, and not hearers only, deceiving your own selves. For if any be a hearer of the word, and not a doer, he is like unto a man beholding his natural face in a glass: For he beholdeth himself, and goeth his way, and straightway forgetteth what manner of man he was. But whoso looketh into the perfect law of liberty, and continueth *therein,* he being not a forgetful hearer, but a doer of the work, this man shall be blessed in his deed." (King James Version, 2012, James 1:22-25) Now, let's look at those same verses in the New Century Version: "Do what God's teaching says; when you only listen and do nothing, you are fooling yourselves. Those who hear God's teaching and do nothing are like people who look at themselves in a mirror. They see their faces and then go away and quickly forget what they looked like. But the truly happy people are those who carefully study God's perfect law that makes people free, and they continue to study it. They do not forget what they heard, but they obey what God's teaching says. Those who do this will be made happy." (New Century Version, 2005, James 1:22-25)

I cannot stress hard enough how important it is to not just read the Bible, but to study it and apply it to our lives. Again, remember the acronym:

- B = Basic
- I= instructions
- B = Before
- L= Leaving
- E = Earth

Chapter Questions

1) What did you get out of this lesson?
2) Is it good enough to only read the Bible? Why or why not, give Bible verses to back this up.
3) Can one grow spiritually without studying the Bible? Why or why not, give Bible verses to back this up.
4) What is the acronym for Bible?
5) Finish this sentence: If we don't study.......
6) What would you say is the most important reason for studying the Bible?
7) Studying the Bible can be compared to what?
8) If Christians were really honest, they would say they are ashamed because why?
9) Does studying the Bible help us in our walk with God? Why or why not, give Bible verses to back this up. Or a personal experience.
10) What is the one Bible verse that you read in this chapter that stepped on your toes the most and why?

References

Lockman Foundation, 1987, Amplified® Bible, Retrieved October 17, 2012, from http://www.biblegateway.com

Thomas Nelson, Inc, 2005, New Century Version, Retrieved October 17, 2012, from http://www.biblegateway.com

Metrolyrics, n.d., Dust on the Bible Lyrics, Hank Williams Sr. Par. 1-2) Retrieved October 17, 2012, from http://www.metrolyrics.com/dust-on-the-bible-lyrics-hank-williams.html

Got question, 2011, Why read/study the Bible, 2011, Retrieved October 18, 2012, from http://www.gotquestions.org/why-read-Bible.html

plagiarism. (n.d.). *Collins English Dictionary - Complete & Unabridged 10th Edition*. Retrieved October 20, 2012, from Dictionary.com website: http://dictionary.reference.com/browse/plagiarism

Meyers M., 2012, doctrine, E-Sword, Version 10.1 Computer Software, Strong's dictionary, Retrieved October 19, 2012

Meyers M., 2012, inspiration, E-Sword, Version 10.1 Computer Software, Strong's dictionary, Retrieved October 18, 2012

Chapter Two the Bible

We have covered why study it, but now I think we should understand a little about this book that we call the Holy Bible or the Holy Scriptures.

First off, this chapter cannot cover all the information that there is on the topic of the Bible, but it is my prayer that it gives you enough information that it builds your faith in the Word that changes your life.

I wanted to start with all these amazing facts about the Bible however, I decided to talk about my personal experience with the Bible.

The truth is, I would not be where I am today if it were not for the Bible and Jesus. When I first totally surrendered my life over to Lord, I tried to study the Bible however, I struggled with understanding it and because of that, it made it hard for me to grow in the Lord and made me frustrated to the point where I gave up.

Now don't get me wrong here, I did not stop believing in God; I just felt like why bother if I can't understand it. Because of that attitude not only did I stop trying to study the Bible eventually other things started to get put on the backburner as well like going to church, praying and going to youth programs. Needless to say , because of all that, my life went down a dark path, but praise God He does not give up on us.

When I was 20, my life was in a tail spin. I was married to an abusive wife; I was drunk or stoned most of the time and the times I was not doing those things, I was in and out of clinical depression and getting in trouble with the law. Finally, God put into my life a pastor who really understood the Biblical teaching of love and so did his church.

Well, I got into trouble with the law and was told I had to do community service and I did it at this pastor's church. He only had one condition and that was that I come to church at least once. I agreed and went and the love that was shown me blew me away and I was compelled to keep going. Finally, I gave in and totally rededicated my life to Jesus.

The problem was I still was having trouble understanding the Bible and I broke down .My pastor asked what was going and I felt like a failure all over again. He asked what Bible I was using; I was like umm the King James (To tell you the truth I did not know there were other translations out there.) He told me about some different translations. I went to the Christian book store and told them what was going on and they put into my hands the Bible that turned everything around for me, it was the New Century Version. (That is one of the reasons why I use it in this book.)

Boy, I dug into the Word and ate it up like it was candy. Like I said earlier, I was like a kid in a candy shop that was told he could have all he wanted. I was learning so much and just learning it made me feel so great.

As I started to apply the Bible to my life, things really started to change for me. Yes, I still had to go through some things like my divorce, but then God brought into my life a woman that is a Christian and we have a wonderful marriage. The thing is if it was not for the Bible and taking the time to study it and apply it to my life, my life would not be where it is today.

The bottom line is this: I tried the Bible and it works , that is all that matters. Every time I have put it to the test it came through for me, or I should say, God kept His word. I had to find out that the Word was not just God's word for how to live our lives, but that it was also His promises. Once I got that into my head and spirit, things started to really change for me. I can go on and on about how the Bible and God changed me, but I think we should look at some other things.

The Bible

The Bible is for the Christian, the final authority with everything. You might say Christians go by: "If God said it {Meaning the Bible} I believe it and that settles it." With Christians, anything from sex to marriage to literally everything, we go to the Bible.

Christianity stands or falls on three facts: 1} The Bible being trustworthy, 2} Jesus Christ's Deity and 3} the death, burial and resurrection of the Lord Jesus Christ. Why is the Bible first? Because if the Bible can be proven unreliable, everything that every Christian believes will crumble. However; if the opposite is true, then Christianity has a basis to stand. Dan Story, author of "Defending Your Faith" wrote "If the Bible can sustain its truth claims in the areas in which can be investigated, then it is reasonable to trust it in spiritual matters."(Story, 1992, p. 34)

Uniqueness of the Bible

The authors came from various backgrounds. Moses, who wrote the first five, books of the Bible called the Pentateuch, was trained in the best schools in Egypt, Peter was a fisherman, Joshua was a military general, Matthew a tax collector, Daniel, a prime minister, Luke, a doctor. Also, to add to the uniqueness of the Bible , is where the books were written. Moses wrote the Pentateuch in the wilderness, Jeremiah was written in a dungeon, Paul, inside prison walls, John, while on exile, in the Isle of Patmos. It was written on 3 continents: Asia, Africa and Europe, in three different languages, Hebrew, Aramaic and Greek.

The Bible is also uniquely different due to the fact of it being uniquely translated. The Bible is one of the first major books translated from Hebrew into Septuagint Greek, around 250 BC. The Bible has been translated and retranslated and paraphrased more than any other book in existence. (Boa,2012,Para,3)

> Let's look at the uniqueness of the Bible.
> It has been reported for about 50 years that the Bible has been the largest seller of all books published in the history of the world. The Bible was written by about 40 men in about 1600 years, dating from 1500 B.C. to about 100 A.D. These men wrote as they were moved by the Holy Spirit (2 Pet. 1:21). They wrote not in words of human wisdom but in words taught by the Holy Spirit (1 Cor. 2:13). (Slick, 2012, Para.1)

> The individual writers, at the time of writing, had no idea that their message was eventually to be incorporated into such a Book, but each nevertheless fits perfectly into place and serves its own unique purpose as a component of the whole." (Clark, Morris, 1987, Unique Structure section, Para. 2)

Can the Bible be Trusted?

One of the questions I get when teaching on how to study the bible is; can the Bible be trusted? The answer is a loud yes and not just because the Bible said so or that I take it on faith, but the fact that there is proof out there to back up the Bible.

As Christians, we take the Bible by faith and we believe it however, we do not do so on blind faith. The one thing that upsets me more than anything else is when people say you have to have blind faith and they use this verse: John 20:29 "Jesus saith unto him, Thomas, because thou hast seen me, thou hast believed: blessed *are* they that have not seen, and *yet* have believed." (King James Version, 2012, 1 Pet. 3:15) They are taking this verse out of context because Jesus was not talking about believing the Bible on blind faith, but believing because they have not seen Him like Thomas did. To be honest ,He was in a way scolding Thomas for not believing what Jesus said would happen.

We need to have faith in God and His word, but that does not mean blind faith. If we were to have blind faith then why did Jesus use many infallible proofs? Acts 1:3 Not only that, the fact is, there are so many proofs out there to back up the Bible, I have to ask; why are we to take it on blind faith? In fact, Jesus said this: if the blind lead the blind the two will fall into a ditch Matt 15:14. Think about it, if we were to have blind faith then we would have to believe blindly every doctrine that is out there, because if faith was blind, we would not be able to tell the true doctrine from the false.

If faith is so blind, then why do we see it working every day? We can see faith working in the lives of fellow believers and in ours when we do the Word and have faith in it and it produces results that in itself is proof that the Bible is true.

Does the Bible teach blind faith? The answer is no, it does not; in fact, it teaches us just the opposite. Look at this verse: 1Th 5:21 "Prove all things; hold fast that which is good." (King James Version, 2012, 1 Th. 5:21) Now look at it in the New Century Version "But test everything. Keep what is good" (New Century Version, 2005, 1 Th. 5:21)

I think it is clear that we don't live on blind faith, in fact the Bible says we are to walk by faith not by sight right? But how can we walk with our eyes shut? We can't, what this verse is getting at is even though we can see things right? We have to trust that God will work it out, but we know that from things in our past and others.

Folks, faith is anything but blind and if you're walking blindly, open your eyes you might see you have been going in the wrong direction. So with that said, let's get into some things that show we can trust the Bible.

Facts

The accuracy of the Bible will come to light under these truths. One: We have more manuscripts of the New Testament than any other literature in history, Two: The care that was taken when copying the Bible is surpassed by no other, Three: Outside sources show the Bible to be accurate and Four: Internal evidence.

Internal evidence

Well, let me ask you something: If I said something was going to happen and it did, would that be proof that what I said was true and that I could be trusted? Of course it would be and if I was able to do that more than once and be right every time the more I could be trusted.

The Bible can be trusted then because it has more fulfilled prophecies than any other religious document out there. "There are 26 other religious books that people of faith believe are divinely inspired (the Hindu Vedas, the Quran, the Book of Mormon, etc.). Of these twenty-six books, none of them contain any specific, fulfilled prophecies. None." (Campbell, 2012, Fulfilled Prophecies section, para. 1)

Now think about this, there are over 400 prophecies concerning the Messiah and Jesus fulfilled every one of them , right down to the smallest detail. This is not only amazing, but it is astronomical meaning impossible for one man to do it however, one man (Jesus) did do it. Now, keep in mind too that these prophecies were made hundreds and thousands of years before Jesus came on the scene.

Let's take the time to look at just a few of these and where they were fulfilled.

1) Seed of woman Gen. 3:15
    a. Fulfilled Matt. 1:18 & Luke 1:35
2) Born of a virgin Isa. 7:14
    a. Fulfilled Matt. 1:18 & Luke 2:7
3) Great men coming to adore Ps. 72:10
    a. Fulfilled Matt. 2:1-11
4) Working miracles Isa. 35:5-6
    a. Fulfilled Matt. 11:4-6 & John 11:47
5) Disciples forsaking Him Zech. 13:7
    a. Fulfilled Matt. 26:31, 56
6) Betrayed by a friend Ps. 41:9; 55:12-14
    a. Fulfilled John 13:18,21
7) His death Zechariah 12:10
    a. Fulfilled John 19:34, 37

Here we have just a few of the prophecies of the Christ and Jesus fulfilled every one of them even right down to the smallest detail that was said about Him in the Old Testament. As I said earlier, the odds of one man doing this is astronomical.

One of the comebacks that I and others get is that Jesus could have manipulated the prophecies. The problem with that is a few he could have, but all 400, give me a break. There is no way Jesus could have manipulated. Let's just look at a few of these.

It was prophesied that the Christ would be born in Bethlehem Mic. 5:2 and this was fulfilled in Matt. 2:1 & Luke 2:4-6 by Jesus. Now there is no way Jesus could have told Mary "Ok, hurry up now, got to get to Bethlehem." any more than we had any choice in where we were born.

It was prophesied that Great men would come to adore Ps. 72:10 and was fulfilled in Matt. 2:1-11. Now, could you just see Jesus send out a letter to these 3 men? “Ok, come and adore me, I am born. Now take into consideration that Jesus did not know these men and that Jesus was only about 2 years when they came. Not to also mention that they had stopped and talked to Herod to find out where Jesus was.

Not only do we have the prophecies in the Bible, we also have the unity of the Bible and what I mean by this is the fact that there is no contradiction in the Bible. “The Bible covers hundreds of topics, yet it does not contradict itself. It remains united in its theme.” (Zukeran, 2012, Unity section, para. 2)

Josh McDowell said in his book called Evidence That Demands a Verdict

> Biblical authors spoke on hundreds of controversial subjects with harmony and continuity form Genesis to Revelation. There is one unfolding story: "God's redemption of man." He also goes on to say:
> Take ten contemporary authors and ask them to write their viewpoints on one controversial subject. Would they all agree? No, we would have disagreements from one author to another. Now look at the authorship of the Bible. All these authors, from a span of fifteen hundred years, wrote on many controversial subjects, and they do not contradict one another (McDowell, 1979, pp.16, 17)

The fact is the Bible itself proves that it is reliable however, for some that is not good enough and in a way I can understand where they are coming from, but the Lord has made sure that is more evidence than that so now let’s look at outside sources.

Outside Sources

For me, one of the most convincing proofs to back up the Bible is archaeology. One of the reasons I say this is because of the fact that it validates some of the stories that are in the Bible. If I come to you and told you that in Egypt women played a game called cat and mouse and you did not believe me but, later found out that they uncovered a game in Egypt called cat and mouse and records showing that women played the game would you believe me then? Of course you would and that is what archaeology does for the Bible.

Nelson Glueck - "It may be stated categorically that no archaeological discovery has ever controverted a biblical reference." (Nelson, 1959, pp. 31-32)

William F. Albright - "There can be no doubt that archaeology has confirmed the substantial historicity of Old Testament traditions." (Albright, 1956, p. 176)

Miller Burrows former professor of archaeology at Yale wrote: - "On the whole … archaeological work has unquestionably strengthened confidence in the reliability of the Scriptural record. More than one archaeologist has found his respect for the Bible increased by the experience of excavation in Palestine. Archaeology has in many cases refuted the views of modern critics." (Bannister, 2912, The External Test para. 1)

Archeology proves the Old Testament

Archeologists discovered the walls of Jericho in the 1930's and the fact that they were pushed out, not in, like one would think in fact this was such a great discovery that those involved signed a statement that walls were indeed pushed out. (McDowell, 1979, p.69)

> In addition to Jericho, places such as Haran, Hazor, Dan, Megiddo, Shechem, Samaria, Shiloh, Gezer, Gibeah, Beth Shemesh, Beth Shean, Beersheba, Lachish, and many other urban sites have been excavated, quite apart from such larger and obvious locations as Jerusalem or Babylon. Such geographical markers are extremely significant in demonstrating

> that *fact*, not *fantasy*, is intended in the Old Testament historical narratives; otherwise, the specificity regarding these urban sites would have been replaced by "Once upon a time" narratives with only hazy geographical parameters, if any. (Maier, 2004, Biblical Cities Attested Archaeologically section, para. 1)

The fact is, archaeology does nothing, but support the Bible time and time again and cannot be refuted. In fact, look at this quote Hans Kung put it nicely:

> Lay people are usually unaware that the scrupulous scholarly work achieved by modern biblical criticism … represented by scrupulous academic work over about 300 years, belongs among the greatest intellectual achievements of the human race. Have any of the great world religions outside of the Jewish-Christian tradition investigated its own foundations and its own history so thoroughly and impartially? None of them has remotely approached this. The Bible is far and away the most studied book in world literature. (Bannister, 2012, The Historian and the Bible section, para. 2)

> The Care That Was Taken In Copying The Bible
> F.F. Bruce, a well-respected biblical scholar: The Masoretes wrote with the greatest imaginable reverence, and devised a complicated system of safeguards against scribal slips. They counted, for example, the number of times each letter of the alphabet occurs in each book; they pointed out the middle letter of the Pentateuch and the middle letter of the whole Hebrew Bible, and made even more detailed calculations than these. (Bruce, 1963, p. 117)

Let me say this, the care that was taken when copying the Bible is surpassed to any other document. I remember when I had to study this out for my Biblical hermeneutics class, I was like blown away by it all. I guess I did not realize how much work went into it.

I think it would be safe to say that with as much care that went into copying the manuscripts, one can safely say that the manuscripts we have today are no different than the one Moses and the other writers wrote those many years ago.

> The scribes who did the copying of the Old Testament were very meticulous in regard to providing an exact duplicate of the original document. One group of scribes, known as the Masoretes, set its standards much higher than all the other scribes. The Masoretes counted every single letter, word, and verse of the Old Testament in order to preserve its accuracy. (Harrub, n.d., Old Testament section, para. 2)

Harrub goes on to say:

> One scroll found in the Dead Sea caves was of particular importance. It was a scroll of the book of Isaiah—from which only a few words were missing! What was amazing about this scroll was that, when it was compared to the text of Isaiah produced 900 years after it, the two matched almost word for word! Thus, we can be confident that the Old Testament we hold in our hands today is worded exactly as the original writers wrote it.

Let's look at one more thing about copying the Old Testament.

Samuel Davidson was an Irish biblical scholar who tells us of some of the detail that went into copying the Old Testament and they are:

1. A synagogue roll must be written on the skins of clean animals,
2. Prepared for the particular use of the synagogue by a Jew.

3. These must be fastened together with strings taken from clean animals.
4. Every skin must contain a certain number of columns, equal throughout the entire codex.
5. The length of each column must not extend over less than 48 or more than 60 lines; and the breadth must consist of thirty letters.
6. The whole copy must be first-lined; and if three words be written without a line, it is worthless.
7. The ink should be black, neither red, green, nor any other color, and be prepared according to a definite recipe.
8. An authentic copy must be the examplar, from which the transcriber ought not in the least deviate.
9. No word or letter, not even a yod, must be written from memory, the scribe not having looked at the codex before him …
10. Between every consonant the space of a hair or thread must intervene;
11. between every new parashah, or section, the breadth of nine consonants;
12. Between every book, three lines.
13. The fifth book of Moses must terminate exactly with a line; but the rest need not do so.
14. Besides this, the copyist must sit in full Jewish dress,
15. wash his whole body,
16. not begin to write the name of God with a pen newly dipped in ink,
17. Should a king address him while writing that name he must take no notice of him."

Davidson adds that "The rolls in which these regulations are not observed are condemned to be buried in the ground or burned; or they are banished to the schools, to be used as reading books." (McDowell, 1979, p.53)

As a result, I believe with all my heart that the Old Testament in our Bible today is identical to the ones that Moses and the other writers of the Old Testament wrote.

The New Testament

We have talked a lot about the Old Testament, but what about the New Testament, can it be as trustworthy as the Old Testament? The answer is yes it can and just like the Old Testament there is ample proof for this.

Historiography

Now, I know I am trying to keep big confusing words out of this book, unfortunately I cannot do it completely, but I will do my best to make it clear.

Historiography means

1) The body of literature dealing with historical matters; histories collectively.
2) The body of techniques, theories, and principles of historical research and presentation; methods of historical scholarship.
3) The narrative presentation of history based on a critical examination, evaluation, and selection of material from primary and secondary sources and subject to scholarly criteria.
4) An official history: medieval historiographies. (Historiography, n.d., dictionary.com)

Let me try and put this a little simpler: it is the study of any historical document to see if it is trustworthy to be considered true or accurate in its information.

Now, to do this job well, one has to apply something called the Bibliographical test. Now this has nothing to do with the Bible, but how all historical documents are tested.

When it comes to the reliability and trustworthiness of any piece of literature, it must be tested with the same test. In other words, it is unfair to give one test to one and a different test to another. This is true when it comes to the Bible. We must give it the same test as we would to a piece of literature by Shakespeare. Otherwise, it is unfair and nothing can be found trustworthy or reliable.

Apart of the historiography is a test called Bibliographical test. This test will answer three questions for us: how reliable are the copies we currently have? How can we be sure that the documents we have, are accurate copies of the originals? How can we be sure that there have not been significant changes or errors made in the process of copying over the years? These questions are answered when we answer two questions

1. How many copies of the document in question are available and what variances exist between the copies?
    a. This enables us to compare the copies with each other. The more copies we have the better the comparisons that we can make. If the copies of a document are filled with significant differences, then it would not be possible to know what the original author wrote! But if the variances are few and minor, then the process of copying over the years has been faithful to the original.
2. What length of time passed between the original and the earliest copies?
    a. If the earliest copies we have were written hundreds of years after the original, a lot of changes could have been made and we wouldn't know about it. But a short interval of time would increase our assurance in the reliability of the copies (Helsby, 2012, Bibliographical test section, para.2)

So the first question that needs to be ask is what is the timeline between the original and the copies in other words how long from the time the original to when it was copied. This is how it works the closer the copy is to the original the more reliable the copy is.

Here comes in the problem with this question and that is the material that was used would break down rather fast and therefore they had to be recopied rather fast. The paper for the New Testament was written on papyrus (puh-PIE-rus)

1. A tall, aquatic plant, Cyperus papyrus, of the sedge family, native to the Nile valley: the Egyptian subspecies, C. papyrus hadidii, thought to be common in ancient times, now occurs only in several sites.
2. A material on which to write, prepared from thin strips of the pith of this plant laid together, soaked, pressed, and dried, used by the ancient Egyptians, Greeks, and Romans.
3. An ancient document, manuscript, or scroll written on this material. (papyrus, n.d., para.)

So because of that, we don't have any of the original, therefore we have to have some test that we can do so we can tell if it is what they actually wrote back 2000 years ago and that is timeline between the original and the copies.

Let us deal with question one: how many copies of the document in question are available and what variances exist between the copies?

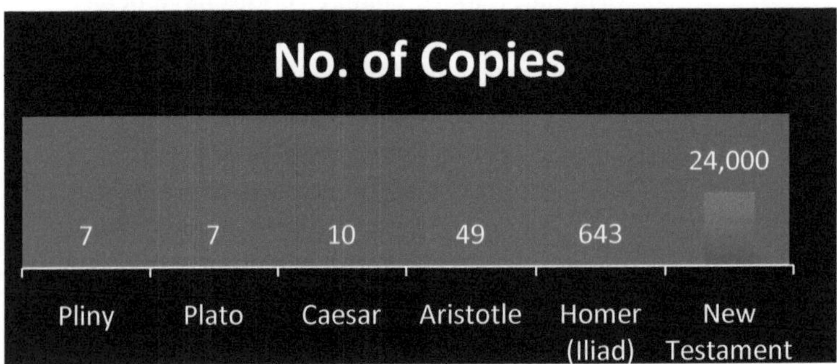

As we can see we have more copies of the New Testament than we do for any other work of literature. With 24,000 copies that is a significant amount to compare to one another to see if there are a major amount of discrepancies. One would think that even with that many copies that they all cannot agree 100% and guess what ,they don't however, let's take a look at something.

If I told you that I was drinking a non alcoholic beer with alcohol in it would you say that it was still non alcoholic? I am sure you would say no however, what if I said that the alcohol is 0.50% by volume? (http://beeradvocate.com, 2012) Now compare that to what a real bottle or can of alcohol has in it and that is anywhere from 4.2% to 8.0% (http://alcoholcontents.com/beer/) now that 0.50% is so small of amount that it does not even matter. In other words, it won't do anything to you and in fact a miner can buy it. Simply put, the amount of alcohol is so small that it does not matter.

However, what does this have to do with the New Testament and the fact that they don't agree 100%? Good question and I am glad that you asked it and here is the answer. Just like with the non alcoholic beer, the amount that does not agree is so small it does not really matter. Look at what Matt Slick said

These various manuscripts, or copies, agree with each other to almost 100 percent accuracy. Statistically, the New Testament is 99.5% textually pure. That means that there is only 1/2 of 1% of all the copies that do not agree with each other perfectly. But, if you take that 1/2 of 1% and examine it, you find that the majority of the "problems" are nothing more than spelling errors and very minor word alterations. For example, instead of saying Jesus, a variation might be "Jesus Christ." So the actual amount of textual variation of any concern is extremely low. Therefore, we can say that we have a remarkably accurate compilation of the original documents. (Slick, 2012, hasn't the Bible been rewritten so many times that we can't trust it anymore? para. 2)

So now that we have dealt with the amount of copies that we have and the accuracy of them let us now look at the time passed between the original and the earliest copies.

Author	Date Written	Earliest Copy	Time Span
Pliny	61-113 A.D.	850 A.D	750 yrs

Plato	427-347 B.C.	900 A.D	1200 yrs
Caesar	100-44 B.C.	900 A.D.	1000
Homer (Iliad)	900 B.C.	400 B.C	500 yrs
New Testament	40-100 A.D.	125 A.D.	25 yrs

The reason why this is so important is the fact that the closer the copy is to the original the more trustworthy it is. Let me try and help you to understand this better. If I write a letter to my wife and a year later she copies it and because she did it so soon there is less chance of the original being degraded however, if she waits 50 years; now letters have been rubbed off or smudged or pieces have been ripped off from wear and tear and she copies it, is it going to look like the original? No, of course not, now instead of reading I love you so much but hate it when people tease you, she is going to read I love you so much but I hate you. The same is true with manuscripts; because they were copied much closer to the time of the originals, there was less chance of corruption or deterioration, therefore making the copies even more reliable and trustworthy.

I will deal with one last thing here because it seems to be a common misconception and that is this: the Bible was written in one language, translated to another language, then translated into yet another and so on until it was finally translated into the English.

The complaint is that since it was rewritten so many times in different languages throughout history, it must have become corrupted. Kind of like the old game that we did in school called the telephone game, the teacher would whisper something in a kid's ear and they would whisper to the next and so on and so forth to the last kid and by the time it got to them, the story has changed from I got a brown dog for my birthday to I got a brown dog with spots from Mars for my fishing trip. Ok maybe not that extreme, but you get the point.

> The only problem with this analogy is that it doesn't fit the Bible at all. When we translate the Bible, we do not translate from a translation of a translation of a translation. We translate from the original language into our language. It is a one-step process and not a series of steps that can lead to corruption. It is one translation step from the original to the English or to whatever language in which a person needs to read. So we translate into Spanish from the same Greek and Hebrew manuscripts. Likewise, we translate into the German from those same Greek and Hebrew manuscripts as well. This is how it is done for each and every language into which we translate the Bible.
>
> We do not translate from the original languages to the English, to the Spanish, and then to the German. It is from the original languages to the English, or into the Spanish, or into the German. Therefore, the translations are very accurate and trustworthy in regards to what the Bible originally said. (Slick, 2012, Hasn't the Bible been rewritten para. 3)

I would like to end this chapter with why I took the time to add it. As I said, in the beginning of this chapter "it is my prayer that it gives you enough information that it builds your faith in the Word that changes your life." However, there is more to it than that.

When I first got saved, I have to admit the Devil plagued my thoughts with how do you know the Bible is true and doubts about if what they said was really what they said and so on. It was from studying about the Bible itself that put all my doubts to rest. I found that I had good reason to believe the Bible and I did not need to take it on blind faith, I had a firm ground to trust the Bible.

This is what I wanted to do for you; maybe you have doubts about the Bible just like I did and I pray that this chapter put those doubts to rest for you.

Chapter Questions

1. What is Bibliographical test?
2. The Bible is for the Christian, the final what? And why?
3. Can the Bible be trusted?
4. Christianity stands or falls on what three facts?
5. What are some of the ways the Bible is unique?
6. List five laws they had to follow in copying the Old Testament?
7. William F. Albright said what about archaeology?
8. Should we as Christian take things on blind faith, why or why not?
9. The Bible can be trusted because it has more what than any other religious book?
10. The accuracy of the Bible will come to light under what truths?
11. How many copies of the New Testament do we have?
12. What is the time span between the originals and the copies?
13. Why is that important?
14. Was the Bible translated into different languages before English?
15. Is the Bible 100% textually pure and if not does it matter?

References

Slick M.,2012, Miscellaneous Information About The Bible, Retrieved October 21, 2012, from: http://carm.org/miscellaneous-information-about-bible
Slick M.,2012, Hasn't the Bible been rewritten so many times that we can't trust it anymore?, Retrieved October 27, 2012, from: http://carm.org/hasnt-bible-been-rewritten-so-many-times-we-cant-trust-it-anymore
Story D., 1997, Defending Your Faith. Published by: Kregel, Inc, Grand Rapids, Mi.

Boa K.,2012, Uniqueness of the Bible, Retrieved October 22, 2012, from: http://bible.org/seriespage/uniqueness-bible

Bruce F.F., 1959, Archaeological Confirmation of the New Testament, Carl F.H. Henry, ed., Retrieved October 22, 2012, from http://www.biblicalstudies.org.uk/pdf/rev-henry/20_nt-archaeology_bruce.pdf

Campbell C., 2012, Can We Trust the Bible?, Retrieved, October 23,2012, from: http://www.alwaysbeready.com/index.php?option=com_content&view=article&id=99&Itemid=43

Thomas Nelson, Inc, 2005, New Century Version, , Retrieved October 22, 2012, from http://www.biblegateway.com

Bannister A., 2012, The Historian and the Bible, Retrieved, October 24,2012, from: theocca.org/news/why-trust-the-bible

Zukeran P., 2012, Authority of the Bible, Retrieved October 23, 2012, from: http://www.leaderu.com/orgs/probe/docs/auth-bib.html
McDowell J., 1879 Evidence That Demands a Verdict Vol. 1, Published by: Campus Crusade, San Bernardino, CA
Nelson G., 1959, Rivers in the Desert, published by: Grove Press, New York

Albright W., 1956, Archaeology and the Religions of Israel. Johns Hopkins University Press, Baltimore, MD

Bannister A., 2012, Why Trust the Bible, Retrieved October 23, 2012, from: http://www.theocca.org/news/why-trust-the-bible

Clark M., Morris H., 1987, The Bible Has the Answer, Retrieved October 24, 2012, from: christiananswers.net/q-eden/edn-t003.html

papyrus. (n.d.). *Collins English Dictionary - Complete & Unabridged 10th Edition*. Retrieved October 26, 2012, from Dictionary.com website: http://dictionary.reference.com/browse/papyrus
Maier P., 2004, Biblical Archaeology: Factual Evidence to Support the Historicity of the Bible, Retrieved October 24, 2012, from: http://www.equip.org/articles/biblical-archaeology-factual-evidence-to-support-the-historicity-of-the-bible/
Bruce. F.F., 1963, The Books and the Parchments, London: Pickering & Inglis Ltc., Retrieved October 25, 2012, from: http://irr.org/todays-bible-real-bible
Harrub B., How did We Get the Bible?, Retrieved October 25, 2012, from: http://www.apologeticspress.org/apcontent.aspx?category=105&article=91
historiography. (n.d.). *Collins English Dictionary - Complete & Unabridged 10th Edition*. Retrieved October 25, 2012,

from Dictionary.com website:
http://dictionary.reference.com/browse/historiography
Helsby, R., 2012, The Bibliographical Test, Retrieved
October 26, 2012, from:
http://knowwhatyoubelieve.com/believe/evidence/bibliographical_test.html

Chapter Three: Where to Start

I believe that the number one reason why people don't study is that they really don't know where to start. I mean let's face it, the Bible, in a way can be intimidating with those big words and how Christians can toss around words like trinity, justification, sanctification and many others. Don't get discouraged studying the Bible it's not as hard as you think it is.

Everything is a whole lot easier if we break things down into steps and that is what we are going to. Anytime you take a trip, even if it is to the store, you mentally map out how you are going to go. For example; when I go to the store without thinking about it, my brain is already thinking how to get to the store and if I have more than one place to go, I plan mentally where to start and finish for example: if I am going to go to the store, then to the pharmacy then to the hardware store, I know the order that I am going to take, I am going to stop at the store first and then hardware store last because I can go from there straight home. Well, studying the Bible is no different we need to roadmap our way.

Distraction

So, with that said, every trip starts out at the beginning so that is where we will start. The beginning is not always the easiest part of the trip; you have to do so much just to get on the road. However, with this trip it is just a matter of getting rid of the distraction.

I think the best verse for this is Mat 6:6 "But thou, when thou prayest, enter into thy closet, and when thou hast shut thy door, pray to thy Father which is in secret; and thy Father which seeth in secret shall reward thee openly." (King James Version, 2012, Mat. 6:6) Now I know this verse deals with not making a spectacle out of yourself when you're praying to get man's attention nevertheless, I can't help, but zoom in on the word closet. The reason why, is that the closet would hide you from people and anything else that could be a distraction, let's look at the definition of the word closet it means: “tam-i'-on Neuter contraction of a presumed derivative of ταμίας tamias (a dispenser or distributor; akin to τέμνω temnō, to cut); a dispensary or magazine, that is, a chamber on the ground floor or interior of an Oriental house (generally used for storage or ***privacy,*** a spot for retirement): - secret chamber, closet, storehouse.” (Emphases added) (Meyers, E-Sword (Version 10.1 Computer Software) , 2012, Strong’s dictionary) The word Privacy is what caught my eye here, simply put, so you don’t get disturbed.

However, that is not the only place that we can see to get rid of distraction. The life of Jesus was our example of how we are to live everyday and if we were to take His example we would that He made time to have private time with the Father without distraction. Let us look at some verses.

1. Mat 14:23 And when he had sent the multitudes away, he went up into a mountain apart to pray: and when the evening was come, he was there alone. (King James Version, 2012, Mat. 14:23)
2. Mar 1:35 And in the morning, rising up a great while before day, he went out, and departed into a solitary place, and there prayed. (King James Version, 2012, Mar. 1:35)

Here we can plainly see that Jesus took time to be alone with the Father, even going so far as sending people away, not that He did not love them or that they were not important to Him, but so He could have an intimate moment with the Father.

I like this word intimate because it means having such a personal moment with someone that it is to be kept secret and it brings about a closeness that makes two people feel so connected that they feel that they can be relaxed with each other, that they can share their inner most parts of themselves without fear. When we study the Word of God, we should make it an intimate moment so we will be really open to hear from God through His Word and hear the Holy Spirit teach us in ways we have never had before.

I think that this is one thing that men struggle with a lot is intimacy with God or others. The reason why I say that is because most men are not the touchy feely type. We are very much physical; ask just about any wife or girlfriend and you will get answers like: “My husband doesn’t talk to me” “We just don’t spend quality time together” or “My husband’s Idea of intimacy is having a dinner in front of the T.V. watching football then grabbing me like a cave man.” I believe that a lot of the problem lies in the fact that men don’t first have intimate moments with God.

> Men may also experience difficulties achieving intimacy because of a lack of ‘emotional vocabulary’. Men often feel less able to express the way they are feeling than women, and may feel uncomfortable with discussions about emotions. However, it is important to remember that intimacy is a *skill*, and as such can be learned. (Newton-John and Newton-John, 2009, Difficulties for men in regard to intimacy section, para. 5)

The thing is though, how important is God to you? If we really cherish our relationship with God, we will make time to spend with Him.

I know it is not always easy to get rid of distractions, I mean let’s face it, in this day and age we all seem to moving 100 miles an hour, but we need to slow down and take time to relax and enjoy those that we love and God needs to be first on that list. I mean after all, He did more for us than anyone else ever has or will.

How many times have you been talking with someone and you could tell that they were not even listening to you because you knew that they were being distracted by other people or other things? I am sure all of us have been there many times over. How did that make you feel? If you’re honest you would have to say it hurt and made you angry and you felt less important to that other person right then. Well, I wonder how God feels when we do it to Him remember God has feelings and emotions just like we do.

Many times Jesus said "He who has ears to hear let him hear." It never seems to fail that when we are being distracted we miss something important. How many times have you been asked to do something like go to the store and get some things and did not hear everything and when you get back home the wife is saying you forgot this and this, next time I am writing it down for you? How many times have you sat in church and got distracted by someone whispering in your ear or you're trying to listen to a teaching on the radio and the kids or spouse are trying to talk to you at the same time and you wind up missing something important that could have been the very thing that God was trying to get to that could change things for you.

Now, I know everyone in our lives need us and we need them and we need to be spending time with them as well. However, we cannot be the parent, spouse, child or friend that we need to be if we neglect our time with God. It is through this time that we spend with God that we learn how to be the best we can be as the parent, spouse, child or friend and if they love us, they will understand and encourage us.

We are in control of our schedule therefore , we can change things around, but God should never be penciled in He should have a permanent spot daily. It does not need to be much however, remember the more you put into a relationship is what you will get out. I am reminded of some words from Paul that says: 2Co 9:6 "But this *I say,* He which soweth sparingly shall reap also sparingly; and he which soweth bountifully shall reap also bountifully." (King James Version, 2012, 2 Cor. 9:6)

We are giving God our time and it is a sacrifice because we are giving up things we want to do to spend time with Him. However, we cannot do it reluctantly or with a bad attitude or have the attitude of doing it because we feel it is our obligation. Look at what Paul tells us: 2Co 9:7 "Every man according as he purposeth in his heart, so let him give; not grudgingly, or of necessity: for God loveth a cheerful giver." (King James Version, 2012, 2 Cor. 9:7)

God has always wanted us to do things just because we love Him that is why God gave us free will. Even Jesus told us "if we love Him keep His commandments." (King James Version John 14:15) God never forces Himself on anyone, He is a gentlemen look at Rev 3:20 "Behold, I stand at the door, and knock: if any man hear my voice, and open the door, I will come in to him, and will sup with him, and he with me." (King James Version, Rev. 3:20)

In our fast pace lifestyles today, how can we get rid of the distractions. The answer is, for the most part, simply making some decisions and then following through with them. Let me give you some suggestions.

1. Turn your phones off. Nothing seems to be more distracting at the time you really want peace than the phone and if you are like me, a ringing phone drives you nuts. Just shut it off, if people really want to get a hold of you they will call back.
2. Put a do not disturb sign on your door.
3. Let others know a head of time that you are going to be busy and ask them nicely not to call or come over at that time.
4. Try to make it the same time everyday that works well for you. I know a lot people that push studying in the morning, but not everyone is a morning person. Like me, my brain does not become awake until noon even if I am up at 7 am. lol. So find a time that works for you. Be consistent with time so you and others get use to it however; don't be so ridged that you cannot make for allowances.
5. Try to get your chores out of the way the best you can. You don't want your mind getting off track thinking of things you have to do yet.
6. Shut the T.V. and computers off. If you use the computer to help you study like I do,

keep the internet use strictly to your study helps and search engines.

7. Study in the same spot every day if possible, that way you can keep all your study material together and not have to stop to hunt for them.
8. Nothing can be more distracting than a hungry tummy, so try to eat like an hour before and eat healthy foods which will boost you with enough energy to keep you focused while you study. Also, have a healthy snack by you and something to drink.
9. Tell whoever lives with you that you are about to start studying and could they please keep the noise down.
10. Make sure that the place you are studying in is relaxing; make sure your chair is comfortable.

Attitude

Check your attitude at the door and leave all bad attitudes outside. If our attitude is not right then we are not going to get anything out of our studies.

We Must have a proper attitude of I am going to get something out of this study today. If we don't have that attitude then it is a good bet you will struggle in your studies and get very little out of them.

Also if we come to our studies with a sense of dread or oh man I have to study again we will not get anything out of it. Paul tells us in Php 2:14 "Do all things without murmurings and disputing" The word murmurings means in the Greek a *grumbling:* - grudging. (Meyers, E-Sword (Version 10.1 Computer Software), 2012, Strong's dictionary)

Now Paul tells us in Colossians 3:23 "And whatsoever ye do, do it heartily, as to the Lord, and not unto men" (King James Version Col. 3:23). Our attitude has to be one of energy or enthusiasm and when we have that type of attitude we will get even more than we thought we could out of our study. If we come to our study with a sluggishness or an attitude or no enthusiasm than you will not get much out of it. Remember what you put into something is what you will get out.

Prayer

The Psalmist said in Psalms 119:18 *"Open my eyes that I may see wonderful things in your law"*

Now, I know you are thinking well duh, of course we need to pray however, I believe that this one gets overlooked a lot because we get in a hurry and jump right into things. But, it is one thing we should not overlook or take lightly.

I think one of the problems we have with prayer, is understanding what prayer really is. Prayers are nothing more than communicating with God, Now, when I say that it is nothing more, I am not demeaning prayer, but simply showing that it is simple and nothing difficult. Prayer is talking with the Father like you would with a spouse or a parent or a close friend. Prayers do not need to be long and poetic like some people make them; it can be as simple as Lord, lead me today. However, we need that intimate prayer with God where we open up and bare our soul with Him; you know our sins, hopes, fears, needs and more.

We must remember that the Bible refers to us as His children and as a Father He wants us to open up to Him. The Bible also refers to Christians as the bride and as our husband; God wants us to bare our deepest parts of ourselves with Him.

The life of Christ was all about setting an example for us to live and we read in Eph. 5:1 Eph 5:1 "Be ye therefore followers of God, as dear children" Now this word followers means in the Greek: "an imitator: - follower." (Meyers, E-Sword (Version 10.1 Computer Software), 2012, Strong's dictionary) To put it simpler, we are to be a copycat of Jesus. In other words, if Jesus did, then we need to be doing as well. You can look at it this way too: when I was a kid, I would try to walk in my dad's footsteps and in his shoes because I wanted to be just like him we must be the same way with Jesus, we must walk in His footsteps. Jesus does give us examples of praying in private look at:

1. Mat 14:23 And when he had sent the multitudes away, he went up into a mountain apart to pray: and when the evening was come, he was there alone. (King James Version, 2012, Mat. 14:23)
2. Mar 1:35 And in the morning, rising up a great while before day, he went out, and departed into a solitary place, and there prayed. (King James Version, 2012, Mar. 1:35)

As I said earlier, we can plainly see that Jesus took time to be alone with the Father, even going so far as sending people away, not that He did not love them or that they were not important to Him, but so He could have an intimate moment with the Father.

There is something in prayer that we need to be careful of and that is distractions with prayer. I don't know about you, but when I pray I get distracted not by outside distractions, but from my own thoughts. It never seems to fail that while I am praying that after a while my mind starts to wander and think about other things. I have had people tell me to play Christian music when I pray however; the music becomes a distraction because I wind up getting into the music. So here is a little trick that works well for me. Take short brakes every so often, stand up and stretch, go get some coffee then you can go back to your prayer and studies.

The sad truth is that prayer has taken a backseat to many things and has been reduced to a routine like mealtime, bead time and yes, church and Bible studies. But you just said that we need to pray, yes, that is true however, it should not be a routine of the same prayer. In other words, don't always pray the same thing pray, from your heart, not a memorized prayer.

I know many people think that we are suppose to pray the Lord 's Prayer word for word trying to prove that memorized prayer is ok, however, let us take a look at it. Jesus said in Mat 6:9 "After this manner therefore pray ye:" In other words, pray like this, Jesus did not say pray this. The Lord's Prayer is an outline of how to pray. Even Jesus said in

Matt. 6:7 “But when ye pray, use not vain repetitions, as the heathen *do:* for they think that they shall be heard for their much speaking.” So, we can see right here that Jesus did not want us to pray memorized prayers, but prayers about how we really feel or from the heart.

Now, do I believe that there needs to be some kind of structure in our prayers? Yes, without a doubt, look at what Paul said in 1Co 14:40 “Let all things be done decently and in order.” The word all would include our prayers. Why? Because where there is no order or structure then there is chaos and God is not the God of chaos. So how do we structure our prayers? Go back to the Lord’s Prayer that is the structure we need. (King James Version, 1 Cor. 14:40)

As stated earlier, Jesus tells us to pray like this, not this, so please keep that in mind. Jesus broke the prayer down to make it easy. “The petitions are six; the first three relate more expressly to God and his honour, the last three to our own concerns, both temporal and spiritual.” (Meyers, 2012, E-Sword, Version 10.1 Computer Software, Retrieved October 31, 2012)

We need to start out by uplifting God and seeking His righteousness we see this by paying for His will in our life. So our prayer could start something like this: Father God, you are so great you have all power not only in Heaven, but here on earth as well. Your name is great Jesus that at your name every knee will bow; now that’s power. Lord I pray that your will be done in my life and that you rule my life not me. By doing this, we are fulfilling what Jesus told us to do in Mat 6:33 “But seek ye first the kingdom of God, and his righteousness; and all these things shall be added unto you.” (King James Version, 1 Cor. 14:40) I need to be honest, until I started this book, I did not look at the first part of the Lord’s Prayer this way and when I saw this, I was like wow, I just found some hidden treasure.

The rest of the Lord’s Prayer is seeking our provisions both physically and spiritually. I believe that it would be right to pray the rest of the prayer like this: Father, I know I am not perfect and I have committed sins and I ask that you forgive me and I thank you for that forgiveness because I know you love me and promised me you would if I confess my sins to you; and Lord, for the sins I don't remember, please bring them to my mind so that I may confess them and get them taken care of. Also, Lord, help me to forgive those that have wronged me that I may be more like you. Lord, I am about to study your Word, the spiritual food for my body and I ask that you give me that food, not just at this time but also throughout the day. Lord, please keep me away from temptation; put a hedge of protection around me so that I might not sin, because I want to always do what is right in your sight; in Jesus' name, amen.

As I was looking into prayer, something came into my spirit and it is this: The book of Psalms uses the word Selah which means to pause. We need to do this as we pray, to pause. When we do pause, it gives God time to talk to us and we must remember that communication is a two way street; we talk, then we listen. I firmly believe this is one of the reasons why God said in Psalms 46:10 "be still and know that I am God" It is when we are still that we can really hear the voice of God.

I believe Matt Slick puts it best when he said "Prayer brings humility to the one praying. It admits dependence on God. If we are humble and depend on God, we are more likely to hear His voice. Prayer means that you are seeking divine intervention. It works power to your words. It changes your heart. It moves you closer to God." (Slick, 2012, para. 4)

When I pray before studying, I ask God to teach me, to open my heart, my eyes, to give me understanding, for guidance, to help me apply to my life and teach others what I have learned. We must understand that it is only God who can do these things and if we ask Him, He will do it. John 14:14 "If ye shall ask any thing in my name, I will do it." (King James Version John 14:4)

What to Study?

I believe one of the other problems most people struggle with is what to study. I mean, let's face it; there is so much in the Bible. I know for me when I started to study the Bible I tried to study one book at a time and I struggled with it because it seemed like there was so much and it would take such a long time that I got discouraged. I mean, to be honest with you, some of the books of the Bible are big and sometimes can get boring, especially with all those genealogies. I still have a hard time studying a book say like Genesis, but I do it because I want to get all that God has for me however, sometimes it puts me almost to sleep.

However, there is an answer and I believe that answer is in topical studies. A topical study is simply picking a topic and then studying all that the Bible has to say about it. Like I said, when I first started to study the Bible I got frustrated with studying one book at a time and did not get much out of it. Then God told me to study one topic at a time and as I did, I found that I was getting grounded in the doctrines of the Bible like the trinity, salvation and more. So at the end of this book I am going to show how I do a topical study to give you something that I did not have and that is an example to follow.

Now, I don't want you to get me wrong; both ways are good and we need to do both however, for those that are just starting out and for those who have studied for a while, but struggled as I did, I really suggest that you do a topic study. One of the reasons I suggest this is because you can go to the Christian book store or on the internet and find all kinds of study helps on topics that will help you in a great way.

Another suggestion is character study what I mean by this is studying about the different people in the Bible. Let's face it from looking at the lives of others we can learn a lot. The people in the Bible where no different than we are today they struggled with everything we do and we can learn from them on what to do and what not to do.

> "The Bible does not shy away from presenting both the strengths and weaknesses of those it portrays. This makes the characters in the Bible "practical" in the sense that we can relate to them and educational in the sense that we can learn from their successes and failures." (Why is it important to study the various characters in the Bible,2012, para. 1)

In fact I believe the Bible teaches us to study the people in the Bible because of what Paul said in 1 Cor. 11:1 “Be ye followers of me, even as I also am of Christ.” In other words as we study the people in the Bible we want to do the things they did that made them successful in following God.

Chapter Questions

1. What is the number one reason why people don't study?
2. Would it be easier to study if we break it down into steps why or why not?
3. What verse shows that we must have quiet time with God?
4. Did Jesus ever spend alone time with the Father if yes where in the bible does it show that?
5. Why is it important to have intimate moments with God?
6. Dose God what us to study out of duty or out of love give a reason or reasons for your answer.
7. Getting rid of distractions is simply a matter of what then what?
8. What are five things you can do to limit distractions?
9. If we allow ourselves to be distracted are we getting everything we can out of our study?
10. After getting rid of the distractions what is the next important thing we must do and why?
11. What is prayer?
12. Does God want us to share everything about us with Him?
13. What are some things we can do to help us with our prayers and studies so we are distracted by our thoughts as much?
14. What does Mat Slick say about prayer?
15. The book of Psalms uses the word Selah which means what?
16. Why should we pause as we pray?
17. Does God what us to use repetitions prayers why or why not?
18. What should we ask for what when we pray?
19. What is a topical study?

References

Meyers M., 2012, closet, E-Sword, Version 10.1 Computer Software, Strong's dictionary, Retrieved October 30, 2012

Newton-John R. & Newton-John P., 2009, Men and intimacy, Retrieved October 30, 2012, from: http://www.mensline.org.au/Men-and-intimacy.html
Meyers M., 2012, Matthew Henry's Commentary, Matt 6:9-14, Version 10.1 Computer Software, Strong's dictionary, Retrieved October 31, 2012

Slick M., 2012, Prayer in Apologetics, Retrieved November 1, 2012, from: http://carm.org/prayer-apologetics
Meyers M., 2012, followers, E-Sword, Version 10.1 Computer Software, Strong's dictionary, Retrieved October 19, 2012

Meyers M., 2012, murmurings, E-Sword, Version 10.1 Computer Software, Strong's dictionary, Retrieved October 19, 2012

Chapter Four: Asking Questions

Asking questions is an important part of life, it is by asking questions that we learn about the world around us. If you're a parent, you will be able to relate to what I am about to say. When my two young daughters where growing up, they asked so many questions throughout the day I was thankful for bed time. Many of us have heard the same questions: why is the sky blue? Where do clouds come from? How did you do that dad? So on and so forth, but the thing is, that is how my and your kids learn and without questions, we would never find the answers.

The thing about this though is as we grow older, we tend to stop asking questions for many reasons, but mainly we don't want to sound dumb or ask a dumb question, however, this is nothing more than a pride problem. Just because we ask a question it does not make us dumb, in fact, we are dumb if we don't ask.

I know you are thinking you don't want others to think you are dumb, again that is a pride issue however, have you ever thought that others might be wanting to ask the same thing, but don't for the same reason you don't and if no one asks the question, then nobody learns. Many times the Bible uses the word ignorant and this word in the Greek means: "not to know (through lack of information or intelligence); by implication to ignore (through disinclination): - (be) ignorant (-ly), not know, not understand, unknown". (Meyers, 2012, E-Sword, Version 10.1 Computer Software, Retrieved November, 04, 2012) Now let me put this in old fashion Texas language here: dumb on purpose and this is what we do if we do not take the time to study and ask questions.

All throughout the Bible we see even the saints asking God questions and what happens? Not only do they learn what God wants them to do, but they also receive the blessing of God. The best two verses I can give you to show this is: Mat 7:7-8 "Ask, and it shall be given you; seek, and ye shall find; knock, and it shall be opened unto you: For every one that asketh receiveth; and he that seeketh findeth;

and to him that knocketh it shall be opened." (King James Version, Mat 7:7-8)

Now we need to really get what Jesus is saying here if we ask we will get or in other words you will be blessed if you would only ask. As I was typing this The Holy Spirit reminded me of another verse and that is this in the last part of James it says: "yet ye have not, because ye ask not."

Paul tells us 1Co 14:40 "Let all things be done decently and in order." (King James Version 1 Cor. 14:40) and there is an order to studying the Bible so that we can get the most out of it. This order I believe is asking the right question now there are two forms of questions and they are questions about the passages themselves and personal questions.

Passage Questions

I do not know about you, but I love a good mystery and in any good mystery you have people trying to find out what is going on or who did it. If you watch or read a mystery, you see the way they do this is by asking questions of people so they can get to the truth. Well, the Bible is no different; we must ask the Bible questions in order to find out what it is telling us.

For this section I am taking the questions from Matt Slick and they can be found at http://carm.org/how-interpret-bible However, the example that I give is from my own study.

There are 9 basic questions we want to be asking of the passage and they are:

1. Who wrote or spoke the passage and to whom was it addressed?
2. What does the passage say?
3. Are there any words or phrases in the passage that need to be examined? In other words, do I understand the meaning of the words as they are used?
4. What is the immediate context?
5. What is the broader context in the chapter and book?

6. What are the related verses to the passage's subject and how do they affect the understanding of this passage?
7. What is the historical and cultural background?
8. What do I conclude about the passage?
9. Do my conclusions agree or disagree with related areas of Scripture and others who have studied the passage?

To help you get a better understanding of how this works I will give you an example.

For this example we will be looking at John 3:5 "Jesus answered, Verily, verily, I say unto thee, Except a man be born of water and *of* the Spirit, he cannot enter into the kingdom of God." (King James Version John 3:5)

1. Who wrote or spoke the passage and to whom was it addressed?
    a. John is the writer however, Jesus is speaking and He is answering a question by Nicodemus who was a Pharisee.
2. What does the passage say?
    a. Jesus is simply saying that in order to get to Heaven, we must be born of the water and the Spirit.
3. Are there any words or phrases in the passage that need to be examined? In other words, do I understand the meaning of the words as they are used?
    a. No, not really, however, for this exercise we will look up the word Spirit and it means in the Greek: "Christ's spirit, the Holy spirit" (Meyers, 2012, E-Sword, Version 10.1 Computer Software, Retrieved November, 05, 2012)

4. What is the immediate context?
    a. John 3:1-8 “There was a man of the Pharisees, named Nicodemus, a ruler of the Jews: The same came to Jesus by night, and said unto him, Rabbi, we know that thou art a teacher come from God: for no man can do these miracles that thou doest, except God be with him. Jesus answered and said unto him, Verily, verily, I say unto thee, Except a man be born again, he cannot see the kingdom of God. Nicodemus saith unto him, How can a man be born when he is old? can he enter the second time into his mother's womb, and be born? Jesus answered, Verily, verily, I say unto thee, Except a man be born of water and *of* the Spirit, he cannot enter into the kingdom of God. That which is born of the flesh is flesh; and that which is born of the Spirit is spirit. Marvel not that I said unto thee, Ye must be born again. The wind bloweth where it listeth, and thou hearest the sound thereof, but canst not tell whence it cometh, and whither it goeth: so is every one that is born of the Spirit.” (King James Version John 3:1-8)
5. What is the broader context in the chapter and book?
    a. The whole context of the chapter is all about salvation and what one must do to obtain eternal life. We get this from several verses in this chapter like 3:16-18 and verse 36.

6. What are the related verses to the passage's subject and how do they affect the understanding of this passage?
    a. When I did my search on this verse, this verse came up: 1Pe 3:21 "The like figure whereunto *even* baptism doth also now save us (not the putting away of the filth of the flesh, but the answer of a good conscience toward God,) by the resurrection of Jesus Christ" (King James Version 1 Peter 3:21)
    b. Well, upon first looking at this verse it would seem that the water Jesus was referring to is water baptism, however, is this the case?
    c. We know it cannot be due to the fact that the Bible does not contradict itself and it would because it would contradict many verses like: Rom 3:28 "Therefore we conclude that a man is justified by faith without the deeds of the law." (King James Version Rom. 3:28) and Eph 2:8-9 "For by grace are ye saved through faith; and that not of yourselves: it is the gift of God: Not of works, lest any man should boast." (King James Version Rom. Eph. 2:8-9)
    d. "So any interpretation which comes to the conclusion that baptism, or any other act, is necessary for salvation, is a faulty interpretation." (Does 1 Peter 3:21 teach that baptism is necessary for salvation? 2012, para. 1)
        i. So where does this leave us then?

1. Well, if we were to look at what Peter said, we would see "(not the putting away of the filth of the flesh, but the answer of a good conscience toward God,)" Even though Peter connected water with salvation, he understood that baptism was an expression of our salvation. That is why he said not the removal of dirt, but it is good conscience toward God.

7. What is the historical and cultural background?
    a. At this time Jesus was not well liked by the religious leaders of His day and they were the ones ruling just about everything. They were still under the law and anything that endangered that threatened them and their way of life and that is exactly what Jesus did.
8. What do I conclude about the passage?
    a. Well, keeping everything in its proper context with the next verse John 3:6 "That which is born of the flesh is flesh; and that which is born of the Spirit is spirit." (King James Version John 3:6) We clearly see that we must first be born of the flesh and then of this spirit to get into Heaven.

9. Do my conclusions agree or disagree with related areas of Scripture and others who have studied the passage?
    a. Yes, without a doubt.

Please keep in mind that this is not everything on this topic, but a brief outline and does not cover all the points of biblical interpretation and we will go a little deeper in how to study in the upcoming chapters.

Personal Questions

These questions are designed to get us to think about how we can get the most out of our studies for our personal life. More to the point, how can we grow as a Christian or apply it to our lives.

1. What is God telling me?
2. How am I encouraged and strengthened?
3. Is there sin in my life for which confession and repentance is needed?
4. How can I be changed, so I can learn and grow?
5. What is in the way of these precepts affecting me? What is in the way of my listening to God?
6. How does this apply to me? What will I do about it?
7. What can I model and teach?
8. What does God want me to share with someone?

We must remember that the whole purpose of studying the Bible is so that we can get things out of it to apply to our lives so we can grow: 2 Tim. 3:16 "for instruction in righteousness" (King James Version 2 Tim. 3:16) Paul is telling us that is the reason why need to study. But we also study so we can teach it to others. Looking at what Jesus said in: Mat 28:20 "Teaching them to observe all things whatsoever I have commanded you." (King James Version Mat 28:20) we can clearly see the command to teach.

I really don't think that I need to go into details with these questions however, let me urge you to be honest with your answers otherwise, you are not going to get out what you need. This leads me to ask: if we are not going to be honest with our answers, then why study? I mean the whole purpose is for us to grow and be better Christians and if we are not going to do that, then are we not just wasting our time and God's?

As I said earlier, I don't think I need to get into details, but I do want to go over them briefly as I want you to get the most out of this study book as you can. I think we need to understand too that there is not always going to be an answer to these questions and that is ok, but the ones that can be answered, we must be willing to honestly look at the answer and apply it to our life.

1. What is God telling me?
    a. This is where we start to really humble ourselves and take us out of the way and let God speak to us. Now you might not like what you hear Him say however, this gives us a chance to hear God and learn what we need to grow. "This requires that our will be poured out and surrendered to His." (Krejcir, 2006, FIFTH: Ask the Question: "What is God Telling Me?" section, para. 1)
2. How am I encouraged and strengthened?
    a. Encouragement and strength only come from the Lord and His Word will do that for us.

"His encouragement greatly helps us to see God's Word as real and impacting" (Krejcir, 2006, SIXTH: Ask the Question: "How am I Encouraged and Strengthened?" section, para. 3)

3. Is there sin in my life for which confession and repentance is needed?
    a. This question of course is designed to make you examine yourself. This is where you really need to be honest with yourself and God.
4. How can I be changed, so I can learn and grow?
    a. The Bible clearly tells us in Prov. 1:5-7 "A wise man will hear, and will increase learning; and a man of understanding shall attain unto wise counsels: To understand a proverb, and the interpretation; the words of the wise, and their dark sayings. The fear of the LORD is the beginning of knowledge: but fools despise wisdom and instruction." A truly wise person is one who is not only willing to admit their short comings, but one that is willing to listen to wise counsel and then do something about it. You see, it does no good to get head-knowledge but not apply it to

our lives. Think about this; if you go to school and get all the wisdom from your professors for medicine and you never take it and apply it or put it into practice, what good did all wisdom do you? Absolutely none.

5. What is in the way of these precepts affecting me? What is in the way of my listening to God?
    a. Simply put, what is stopping me from applying this to my life? Is it people, my own pride, fear, so on and so forth? Everyone has things in their lives that stop them from doing what we know we need to do, but like any roadblock, we can get it out of the way and move forward. This might be something simple and we are able to do it right away; other things might take some time however, if you let God help you, it can be done.
6. How does this apply to me? What will I do about it?
    a. This can be a dangerous question because this requires us to be honest with ourselves and we find out if we are just wasting our time and God's.
    b. It also takes from thinking to planning on how to do it, in other words, we start to

make a map or a list of what we have to do to apply it to our life.

7. What can I model and teach?
    a. I have often said the greatest sermon ever preached is one that is lived in front of others. As I have said before, we do not only study to learn about God and what we need to change, but also to teach it to others. Remember, Jesus said go into all the world and teach: Matthew 28:20.
8. What does God want me to share with someone?
    a. Let me say this with a big warning here: any time we talk to others, we need to do it out of love. Remember the words of Paul: If I do not have love I am nothing 1 Cor. 13:2. We must also remember that God does not bring condemnation on people: Rom. 8:1 says "So now, those who are in Christ Jesus are not judged guilty." (New Century Version Rom. 8:1)

I cannot stress this enough, we must remember that the whole purpose of studying the Bible is so that we can get things out of it to apply to our lives so we can grow: 2 Tim. 3:16 “for instruction in righteousness” (King James Version 2 Tim. 3:16) Paul is telling us that is the reason why we need to study. Also, remember what James told us In James 2:18: “Someone might say, "You have faith, but I have deeds." Show me your faith without doing anything, and I will show you my faith by what I do.” (New Century Version James 2:18)

Chapter Questions

1. Asking questions is how we learn about what?
2. What stops us from asking questions?
3. More to the point, what is stopping you from asking questions?
4. If we do not ask questions, we are what?
5. What does it really mean to be ignorant?
6. Did the Bible saints ask questions?
7. Can we just open our Bibles and start studying or should we do it in order?
8. People find answers by what?
9. What are 3 of the passage questions we should ask?
10. What are 3 of the personal questions we should ask?
11. Out of the personal questions, what one or ones do you think you will struggle with the most and why?

References

Meyers M., 2012, ignorant, E-Sword, Version 10.1 Computer Software, Strong's dictionary, Retrieved November 4, 2012

Meyers M., 2012, Spirit, E-Sword, Version 10.1 Computer Software, Strong's dictionary, Retrieved November 5, 2012

Slick M., 2012, How to Interpret the Bible Retrieved November 5, 2012, from: http://carm.org/how-interpret-bible
Krejcir R.J., 2006, Inductive Bible Study Basics, Retrieved November 6, 2012, from:
http://70030.netministry.com/articles_view.asp?articleid=31556&columnid=3801
Thomas Nelson, Inc, 2005, New Century Version, Retrieved November 7, 2012, from:
http://www.biblegateway.com

Chapter Five: Language of the Bible

I know from the sound of this chapter, you are thinking "oh great, this is where things get hard." Well, the truth is, I will try to keep things as simple as possible, but we are going to be learning some big words. However, do not worry; I will do my best to explain things in simple ways. Not only that, I will try as best as I can to give examples so you can prayerfully understand better. Remember, I am of the philosophy that if we cannot understand things, we cannot apply it and then we are wasting our time and all of this will not do us any good; so I will do my best to help you understand.

One of the questions I get asked most I think is: why learn to study, doesn't the Bible say what it means and means what it says? But, is this a true saying? Well, the answer is simply yes and no. We must remember that the Bible uses two different types of language along with genres and genres means "a class or category of artistic endeavor having a particular form, content, technique, or the like: the genre of epic poetry; the genre of symphonic music." (http://dictionary.reference.com/browse/genre)

The two different types of language used are literal and figurative. Basically, what this means is literal means just that; literal is what it says it is what it means, but then there is figurative and what this means is "of the nature of or involving a figure of speech, especially a metaphor; metaphorical and not literal: The word "head" has several figurative senses, as in "She's the head of the company." Synonyms: metaphorical, not literal, symbolic." (http://dictionary.reference.com/browse/figurative)

I will give two examples of these, the best one for literal is John 3:16 that says "For God so loved the world, that He gave his only begotten Son, that whosoever believeth in him should not perish, but have everlasting life." (King James Version John 3:16) This is a literal verse because this literally happened. God did love the world so much that He did send His one and only Son. Now, for figurative, the best one I can give is found in Rev. 13:1 that says "And I stood upon the sand of the sea, and saw a beast rise up out of the sea, having seven heads and ten horns, and upon his horns ten crowns, and upon his heads the name of blasphemy." (King James Version Rev. 13:1) Now, is there going to be a real beast with seven heads and ten horns in the sea somewhere waiting to rise up out of it? No, of course not, so this must mean something else; now I am not going to get into what it means, however, you get my point.

We can find these throughout the Bible, the question then remains, how can we tell one from the other? I have to admit that sometimes this is hard, but this is where we fall back on prayer and let the Holy Spirit teach us. For me, what I do is ask the question: is this something that already took place or can literally take place or is this something that must have a different understanding or meaning, does this sound even possible; if not, then it must be figurative.

Figurative Language

If we were to take everything in the Bible as literal language, then we would have to say that Jesus is a real lamb or that he is a real door because these are words that described Jesus. John the Baptist said John 1:29 "Behold the lamb of God which taketh away the sins of the world" (King James Version John 1:29) Jesus said that He was the door in John 10:9 Is Jesus really a lamb or a door? No, of course not, so these words must have a different meaning symbolic or metaphorical.

> Whenever we read the words of the Bible, we are faced with a choice: Does God intend this passage to be taken literally, or is the meaning symbolic or metaphorical? Is the language used strictly literal or is it a figure of speech? (Morrison, 2012, How to understand the language of the Bible section, para. 2)

Figures of speech are nothing new in fact we use figures of speech in our everyday communications example is like "my brain is just dead today." Or "You smell like roses." So it should not come as a surprise that the Bible uses them and one of the reasons it does is it helps us to remember. Now there are different types of figures of speech and they are: (Morrison, 1994, Figures of Speech in the Bible)

1. Simile
    a. "A figure of speech in which two unlike things are explicitly compared" (http://dictionary.reference.com/browse/simile)
        i. Example: Mat 13:31 "Another parable put he forth unto them, saying, The kingdom of heaven is like to a grain of mustard seed, which a man took, and sowed in his field" (King James Version Mat. 13:31)
2. Metaphor
    a. "A figure of speech in which a term or phrase is applied to something to which it is not literally applicable in order to suggest a resemblance." (http://dictionary.reference.com/browse/metaphor)
        i. Example: Jesus said in John 6:35 John "And Jesus said unto them, I am the bread of life: he that cometh to me shall never hunger; and he that believeth on me shall never thirst."
            1. Upon looking at a Simile and a metaphor one might think that they are the same thing however, they are not. A simile uses words like or as to compare two things to each other just like the example

under simile "The Kingdom of heaven is **LIKE** to a mustard seed" (emphasis added), but a "metaphor is a figure of speech that says that one thing is another different thing. This allows us to use fewer words and forces the reader or listener to find the similarities." (Whitehall, 2011, para. 5) Example would be the party was the bomb. Meaning that that the party was really good.

3. Anthropomorphism
    a. This is a big word and to be honest with you I was like what in the world does this mean? The best answer I found is from Matt Slick who defines the word this way: "Anthropomorphism comes from two Greek words: anthropos (man) and morphe (form). Therefore, anthropomorphism is when God appears to us or manifests Himself to us in human form or even attributes to Himself human characteristics." I will use a few examples from Matt Slicks chart. (Slick, 2012,diagram)
    b. Human actions - changed mind, relented,

i. Exodus 32:14, "So <u>the Lord changed His mind</u> about the harm which He said He would do to His people."
ii. 2 Sam. 24:16, "When the angel stretched out his hand toward Jerusalem to destroy it, <u>the Lord relented</u> from the calamity, and said to the angel who destroyed the people, “It is enough! Now relax your hand!”

c. Human emotions - sorrow, jealousy
    i. Gen. 6:6, "And the Lord was sorry that He had made man on the earth, and He was grieved in His heart."
    ii. Exodus 20:5, "You shall not worship them or serve them; for I, the Lord your God, am a jealous God, visiting the iniquity of the fathers on the children, on the third and the fourth generations of those who hate Me."
d. Human physique - hands, face
    i. Exodus 7:5, "And the Egyptians shall know that I am the Lord, when I stretch out My hand on Egypt and bring out the sons of Israel from their midst.”
    ii. Num. 6:24, "The Lord make His face shine on you, and be gracious to you."
e. Other - Wings
    i. Psalm 57:1, "Be gracious to me, O God, be gracious to me, for my soul takes refuge

in Thee; and in the shadow of Thy wings I will take refuge, until destruction passes by."

4. Words of association
    a. Simply put a word that means something else:
        i. Take the word Godhead used in Col. 2:9 “Col 2:9 “For in him dwelleth all the fulness of the Godhead bodily.” (King James Version, Col. 2:9) The word Godhead too many people including myself means the Trinity.
5. Personification
    a. “The attribution of a personal nature or character to inanimate objects or abstract notions, especially as a rhetorical figure.” (http://dictionary.reference.com/browse/Personification)

i. Really the whole book of Proverbs uses this type of figure of speech, but look at Pro 1:20 "Wisdom crieth without; she uttereth her voice in the streets" (king James Version Pro. 1:20)
    1. Here we see Solomon portraying wisdom as a woman who is passionately pleading or crying out with people to be wise and not to live as fools who will receive the consequence of their foolish actions.

6. Euphemism
    a. The substitution of a mild, indirect, or vague expression for one thought to be offensive, harsh, or blunt. (http://dictionary.reference.com/browse/euphemism)
        i. Gen. 15:15 "You, however, will go to your fathers in peace and be buried at a good old age." Here Abraham was told that he was going to his fathers, this is a euphemism for dying.

7. Hyperbole
    a. This is simply an exaggeration a blowing things out of proportion to make a point.
        i. John 12:19 "The Pharisees therefore said among themselves, Perceive ye how

ye prevail nothing? behold, the world is gone after him." King James version, John 12:19)

1. Obviously not everyone in the world was following Jesus, but the Pharisees angry with Jesus when they saw the large crowd around Jesus the exaggerated about the amount.

Now, there is way more to this and I suggest you find good books on the topic, however, I am trying to give you some kind of overview to get you to start to look for these in the Bible to help you to get the most you can out of your study.

However, I think there needs to be two more figures of speech we need to look at simply because they show how God emphasizes on things that He thinks is important.

1. Anaphora
    a. This simply means when a word or a phrase is repeated several times within the repetition of a word, at the beginnings of successive sentences.
        i. Matt. 5:3-11 "Blessed are the poor in spirit: for theirs is the kingdom of heaven. Blessed are they that mourn: for they shall be comforted. Blessed are the meek: for they shall inherit the earth. Blessed are they which do hunger and thirst after righteousness: for they shall

be filled. Blessed are the merciful: for they shall obtain mercy. Blessed are the pure in heart: for they shall see God. Blessed are the peacemakers: for they shall be called the children of God. Blessed are they which are persecuted for righteousness' sake: for theirs is the kingdom of heaven. Blessed are ye, when men shall revile you, and persecute you, and shall say all manner of evil against you falsely, for my sake.) King James version, Matt. 5:3-11)

2. Polysyndeton
    a. Is the use of "and" more than is grammatically necessary.
        i. Eph 4:31-32 "Let all bitterness, and wrath, and anger, and clamour, and evil speaking, be put away from you, with all malice: And be ye kind one to another, tenderhearted, forgiving one another, even as God for Christ's sake hath forgiven you." (King James Version Eph. 4:31-32)

        ii. In this case God is emphasizing every word so in this case God is saying I emphasizing I want you to get rid of all of these.

> The evidence is clear that parts of the Bible are meant figuratively, and we are rejecting the Word of God if we refuse to consider the possibility of figures of speech. We should not refuse to understand a method the Bible itself uses. (Morrison, 2012, Truth in symbolic language section, para. 7)

As I said earlier, there is way more information on this than I can put in this book, but take the time to dig into this even further, I promise it can only help you to dig out more from the Bible.

Genres

As I stated earlier, genres means: "a class or category of artistic endeavor having a particular form, content, technique, or the like: the genre of epic poetry; the genre of symphonic music." (http://dictionary.reference.com/browse/genre) Simply put genres means different categories kind of like movies or books like: horror, sci-fi, mystery so on and so forth.

The Bible has different genres and within them are even more genres, now don't panic I will do my best to show them to you and explain them as simply as I can.

Old Testament Genres

1. Narrative
    a. It is basically a story such as the story of David and Goliath, Abraham and Isaac and more. In fact 40% of the Old Testament is made up of stories.
        i. Within Narratives there are other genres and they are: (I got this list from (No Author, no date, https://netfiles.uiuc.edu
            1. heroic narrative
            2. epic narrative
            3. tragic narrative
            4. comic narrative
2. Law
    a. The Law is the first five books or the Pentateuch which "comes from a combination of the Greek word penta meaning five and teuchos which can be translated scroll. Therefore it simply refers to the five scrolls which make up the first of three divisions of the Jewish canon." (No Author, no date, what is the Pentateuch?) These first five books are also called the Torah and that simply means the books of the law. These five books of the Bible are: Genesis, Exodus, Leviticus, Numbers and Deuteronomy.
    b. The law however is found is Leviticus and Deuteronomy.
3. Historical
    a. These books are: Joshua, Judges, Ruth, First Samuel, Second Samuel, First Kings, Second Kings, First Chronicles, Second Chronicles, Ezra, Nehemiah, Esther.
        i. I am going to do something here that I was not going to do however; I want you to get the most out of this book as you can. What I am going to

do here is to give you brief overview and I want to thank Matt Slick because he took all the work out of this for us. You can see this at http://carm.org/old-testament-books

   ii. Joshua – First half of Joshua describes the 7-year conquest of the Land of Promise. The last half deals with partitioning the lands to the people.
   iii. Judges – Time of Judges. This was a bad time period. The Israelites did not drive out all the inhabitants of Canaan and began to take part in their idolatry. 7 cycles of foreign oppression, repentance, and deliverance. In the end, the people failed to learn their lesson.
   iv. Ruth – Kinsman redeemer in Boaz, redeeming Ruth, a Moabitess. Speaks of righteousness, love, and faithfulness to the Lord.

b. The next 6 books trace the time from Samuel to the Captivity.
   i. First Samuel – Samuel carries Israel from judges to King Saul.
   ii. Second Samuel – David as King, adultery, and murder.
   iii. First Kings – Solomon, Israel is powerful. Solomon dies, then division of tribes: 10 to the north and 2 to the south.
   iv. Second Kings – The Divided Kingdom. All 19 kings of Israel were bad; therefore, captivity in Assyria (722 B.C.). In Judah, 8 of 20 rulers were good but went into exile too.

v. First Chronicles – A recounting of the history of Israel to the time of Solomon.
vi. Second Chronicles – continued recounting of the life of Solomon, building of temple, to the captivity. History of Judah only.

c. The Next 3 books deal with Israel's Restoration.
    i. Ezra – Cyrus let most of the Jews return to their land of Israel. Zerubbabel led the people (539 B.C.). Ezra returned later with more Jews (458 B.C.) Built the temple.
    ii. Nehemiah – Building the walls of Jerusalem. Nehemiah got permission from the king of Persia to rebuild the walls (444 B.C.). Revival in the land.
    iii. Esther – Took place during chapters 6 and 7 of Ezra. Mordecai. Plot to kill the Jewish people.

4. Poetic books
    a. Job – a righteous man tested by God. Deals with God's sovereignty.
        i. A righteous man tested by God. Deals with God's sovereignty.
    b. Psalms
        i. Consists of 5 divisions. Worship in song. Large variety of subjects.
    c. Proverbs
        i. Practical wisdom in everyday affairs.
    d. Ecclesiastes
        i. All is vanity. The wisdom of man is futility.
    e. Song of Solomon
        i. A song between Solomon and his Shulammite bride, displaying the love between a man and a woman.

5. Prophet
    a. These books are broke up into two divisions The Major Prophets and Minor Prophets Now don't think like I did that one was more important than the other that is not the case. Why the division is simply this that the Major Prophets books are bigger than the Minor Prophet books. It does not mean Samuel is more important than Amos.
        i. Major Prophets
            1. Isaiah, Jeremiah, Lamentations, Ezekiel, Daniel
        ii. Minor Prophets
            1. Hosea, Joel, Amos, Obadiah, Jonah, Micah, Nahum, Habakkuk, Zephaniah, Haggai, Zechariah, Malachi.
    b. Major Prophets
        i. Isaiah
            1. Looks at the sin of Judah and proclaims God's judgment. Hezekiah. Coming restoration and blessing.
        ii. Jeremiah
            1. Called by God to proclaim the news of judgment to Judah, which came. God establishes a New Covenant.
        iii. Lamentations
            1. 5 lament poems. Description of defeat and fall of Jerusalem.
        iv. Daniel
            1. Many visions of the future for the Gentiles and the Jews.

c. Minor Prophets
    i. Hosea
        1. Story of Hosea and his unfaithful wife, Gomer. Represents God's love and faithfulness and Israel's spiritual adultery. Israel will be judged and restored.
    ii. Joel
        1. Proclaims a terrifying future using the imagery of locusts. Judgment will come but blessing will follow.
    iii. Amos
        1. He warned Israel of its coming judgment. Israel rejects God's warning.
    iv. Obadiah
        1. A proclamation against Edom, a neighboring nation of Israel that gloated over Jerusalem's judgments. Prophecy of its utter destruction.
    v. Jonah
        1. Jonah proclaims a coming judgment upon Nineveh's people. But they repented and judgment was spared.
    vi. Micah
        1. Description of the complete moral decay in all levels of Israel. God will judge but will forgive and restore.
    vii. Nahum
        1. Nineveh has gone into apostasy (approx. 125 years after Jonah) and will be destroyed.

viii. Habakkuk
    1. Near the end of the kingdom of Judah, Habakkuk asks God why He is not dealing with Judah's sins. God says He will use the Babylonians. Habakkuk asks how God can use a nation that is even worse than Judah.

ix. Zephaniah
    1. The theme is developed of the Day of the Lord and His judgment with a coming blessing. Judah will not repent, except for a remnant, which will be restored.

x. Haggai
    1. The people failed to put God first, by building their houses before they finished God's temple. Therefore, they had no prosperity.

xi. Zechariah
    1. Zechariah encourages the Jews to complete the temple. Many messianic prophecies.

xii. Malachi
    1. God's people are lax in their duty to God. Growing distant from God. Moral compromise. Proclamation of coming judgment.

New Testament Genres

1. The Gospels
    a. The gospels are the first four books of the New Testament and they are: Matthew, Mark, Luke and John.
        i. The Gospels are narratives however; they differ from the Old Testament narratives in that they are more focused or more centered on life of Jesus. I guess you could say they are a mixture of narratives and history I say that do to the fact that Jesus refers back to the Old Testament many times.
    b. Just like the Old Testament had figures of speech in them so does the Gospel and they are:
        i. Parables
            1) Parables are short stories that make a spiritual point that the everyday person could understand and remember and apply to their life.
            2) Jesus used everyday things that people could relate to. This will just be a small list.
                a. Seed
                b. Sheep
                c. Wine
                d. Vine and branches
            3) Jesus taught more in parables than any other way in fact He gave a total of 50 parables. One of the reasons why is that it was prophesied in the Old Testament that the Messiah would preach in Parables.

a. Psa 78:2 I will open my mouth in a parable: I will utter dark sayings of old: (King James Version)

4) Below is a small list
   a. The parable of the Speck and the log.
      i. Matt. 7:1-6 & Luke 6:37-43
   b. The parable of the two houses.
      i. Matt. 7:24-27 & Luke 6:47-49
   c. The parable of children in the marketplace.
      i. Matt.11:16-17 & Luke 7:32
   d. The parable of the two debtors.
      i. Luke 7:41-42
   e. The parable of the sower.
      i. Matt.13:3-8, Mark 4:3-8 & Luke 8:5-8

ii. Prophetic
    1) Many times throughout the life of Jesus He spoke of things that would take place in the future.
        a. The most famous one is found in Matt. Chapters 24 & 25 known as the Olivet discourse.

iii. Metonymy
    1) A figure of speech that consists of the use of the name of one object or concept for that of another to which it is related, or of which it is a part, as "scepter" for "sovereignty," or "the bottle" for "strong drink," or "count heads (or noses)" for "count people." (http://dictionary.reference.com/browse/metonymy)
        a. Mt 27:4 "having betrayed innocent blood" (King James Version Mt. 27:4)
        b. Mt 16:17 flesh and blood (King James Version Mt. 16:17)
        c. Acts 18:6 Your blood be on your own heads (King James Version Acts 18:6)

iv. Metaphor
    1) A figure of speech in which a term or phrase is applied to something to

which it is not literally applicable in order to suggest a resemblance, as in "A mighty fortress is our God." (http://dictionary.reference.com/browse/Metaphor)

a. Jude 12 they are clouds without water (King James Version Jude 12)
b. Mt 10:38 he who does not take his cross (King James Version Mt. 10:38)

c. As I said earlier, the four gospels are made up of both narrative and history. We have taken a look at the narrative and figures of speech, so now let's look at briefly the history.
    i. Matthew
        1) Matthew wrote to the Jews was that he could show that Jesus had legal claim to the throne of David therefore, making Jesus the King of the Jews. Matthew also starts out with this declaration with the genealogy of Joseph.
    ii. Mark
        1) Presents Jesus as the Servant and proves that Jesus is indeed the Messiah.
    iii. Luke
        1) Presents Jesus as the Son of Man who came to save the lost. Here we find the genealogy of Jesus through Mary.

        iv. John
            1) Here we see that Jesus is indeed God in the flesh the anointed one or the Messiah.
    d. Now, under the historical category, we also have the book of Acts.
        i. Acts
            1) Here we have the ascension of Jesus, the day of Pentecost and the start of the church and the conversion of Paul.
2. Pauline epistles Or the Pauline letters Paul wrote two thirds of the New Testament.
    a. Romans
        i. Here we see examination of justification and sanctification. Justification is also called justification by faith. This is the teaching that the act of God (The sacrifice of Jesus) is how humankind is made or accounted just or free from guilt or judgment of sin. Sanctification means to be growing in Christ that is every day we should look more like Jesus and less like ourselves.
    b. 1 Corinthians
        i. This letter is to the church of Corinth and deals with corrections due to immorality, lawsuits, and abuse of the Lord's Supper and more.
    c. 2 Corinthians
        i. Here we see Paul defending himself to the church in Corinth and the work of preachers and to show that no one is better than the next.
    d. Galatians
        i. Here Paul comes against the Judaizers in the churches of Galatia.

These where people trying to hook Christians back up to the Jewish law. Here we see Paul lifting the legalistic requirements from the believer.

e. Ephesians
    i. This letter was written to the saints that lived in Ephesus. This letter was a manual showing how a Christian should live and the church could be unified and how to deal with spiritual warfare.
f. Philippians
    i. This letter was written to the saints that lived in Philippi. Paul speaks of his imprisonment and encourages those who are in the ministry and thanked for their help and encouragement. He tells to beware them of legalism.
g. Colossians
    i. This letter was written to the saints that lived in Colosse this is one church that most believe Paul never got the chance to visit. Paul had heard about the false teachers troubling the church. Paul reaffirms in that Jesus was indeed the divine Son of God.
h. 1 Thessalonians
    i. This letter is to the church of Thessalonians. Here Paul shows them that the church is founded on two principles faith in Christ and love. Paul encourages believers to sacrifice ourselves through faith, hope and love. Paul also reaffirms in them that Christ will return.

i. 2 Thessalonians
    i. This letter is to the church of Thessalonians. Here Paul was clarifying the misunderstandings the people ha about Jesus' return and to trust in God's judgment.
j. 1 Timothy
    i. Instructions to Timothy on proper leadership and dealings with false teachers, the role of women, prayer, and requirements of elders and deacons.
k. 2 Timothy
    i. A letter of encouragement to Timothy to be strong.
l. Titus
    i. Paul left Titus in Crete to care for the churches there. Requirements for elders.
m. Philemon
    i. A letter to the owner of a runaway slave. Paul appeals to Philemon to forgive Onesimus.
n. Hebrews
    i. A letter to the Hebrew Christians in danger of returning to Judaism. It demonstrates the superiority of Jesus over the O.T. system. Mentions the Melchizedek priesthood. (Hebrews may be of Pauline origin. There is much debate on its authorship). All though it is my belief that Paul is indeed the author of Hebrews.

3. Letters
    a. James
        i. A practical exhortation of believers to live a Christian life evidencing regeneration. It urges self-

examination of the evidence of the changed life.

b. 1 Peter
    i. Peter wrote this letter to encourage its recipients in the light of their suffering and be humble in it. Mentions baptism.
c. 2 Peter –
    i. Deals with the person on an inward level, warnings against false teachers, and mentions the Day of the Lord.
d. 1 John
    i. John describes true fellowship of the believers with other believers and with God. Describes God as light and love. Encourages a holy Christian walk before the Lord. Much mention of Christian love.
e. 2 John
    i. Praise for walking in Christ and a reminder to walk in God's love.
f. 3 John
    i. John thanks Gaius for his kindness to God's people and rebukes Diotrephes.
g. Jude
    i. Exposing false teachers and uses O.T. allusions to demonstrate the judgment upon them. Contends for the faith.
h. Revelation
    i. A highly symbolic vision of the future rebellion, judgment, and consummation of all things.

Chapter Questions

1. Does the Bible say what it means and mean what it says? Why or why not?
2. What are the two different types of language?
3. What are three different types of figurative language? Give examples from the Bible.
4. Give an example of literal language?
5. Is it important to understand the different use of langue in the Bible why or why not?
6. Give three examples of a simile from the Bible.
7. What is Anthropomorphism?
8. What are the different genres of the Old Testament?
9. Is everything in the Bible literal?
10. What is the definition of genres?
11. What are the genres of the New Testament?
12. What are the figures of speech in the New Testament?

References

Morrison M., 2012, Literal and Figurative, Retrieved November 7, 2012, from: http://www.gci.org/bible/literal

Genre. (n.d.). *Collins English Dictionary - Complete & Unabridged 10th Edition*. Retrieved November 07, 2012, from Dictionary.com website: http://dictionary.reference.com/browse/genre

figurative. (n.d.). *Collins English Dictionary - Complete & Unabridged 10th Edition*. Retrieved November 07, 2012, from Dictionary.com website: http://dictionary.reference.com/browse/figurative

simile. (n.d.). *Collins English Dictionary - Complete & Unabridged 10th Edition*. Retrieved November 08, 2012, from Dictionary.com website: http://dictionary.reference.com/browse/simile

Whitehall H., 2011, What is the difference between similes and metaphors?, Retrieved November 8, 2012, from: http://www.putlocker.com/file/6TEBGGUHK72P#

Slick M., 2012, Anthropomorphism: God relates to us in human terms, retrieved November 8, 2012, from: http://carm.org/anthropomorphism-god-relates-us-human-terms

Personification. (n.d.). *Collins English Dictionary - Complete & Unabridged 10th Edition*. Retrieved November 08, 2012, from Dictionary.com website: http://dictionary.reference.com/browse/Personification

euphemism. (n.d.). *Online Etymology Dictionary*. Retrieved November 08, 2012, from Dictionary.com website: http://dictionary.reference.com/browse/euphemism

irony. (n.d.). *Dictionary.com Unabridged*. Retrieved November 08, 2012, from Dictionary.com website: http://dictionary.reference.com/browse/irony

Fee G. & Stuart D., 2003, How to Read the Bible for All Its Worth, Retrieved November 14, 2012, available from: http://www.pdfbook.co.ke

No Author, no date, Genres in Biblical literature, Retrieved November 14, 2012, available from: https://netfiles.uiuc.edu/klee7/www/iccf/docs/blitgenres

No Author, no date, What is the Pentateuch?, Retrieved November 15, 2012, from: http://www.gotquestions.org/Pentateuch.html

metonymy. (n.d.). *Collins English Dictionary - Complete & Unabridged 10th Edition*. Retrieved November 16, 2012, from Dictionary.com website: http://dictionary.reference.com/browse/metonymy

Chapter Six: Interpretation

This is where we are going to start to put it all together. I know this chapter is going to sound complicated, but I promise I will make it easier than it will sound.

The thing that we need to understand is that no one understands the enter Bible from Genesis to Revelation. Anyone who says they do is just puffed up with pride because we have a finite mind trying to understand an infinite mind of God, it just is not going to happen. The Bible tells us in 1Co 13:9 "For we know in part, and we prophesy in part." And 1Co 13:12 "For now we see through a glass, darkly; but then face to face: now I know in part; but then shall I know even as also I am known." (King James Version 1Co 13:9 & 12)

We also need to know that there is no new revelation, what I mean by that is we are not getting anything new from God as far as how to live our lives or anything new about God everything we need to know is in the Bible. However, God does reveal His Word to us or makes His Word clear for us or understandable. In other words, as we study, He teaches us what the Word means. Also, we are not studying the Bible to find something that no one knows, but we are studying to get closer to God and grow in the Lord so we can be productive in our homes, churches, jobs and community.

As I said in the introduction about why I wrote this book, you might be thinking that I wrote this book to help you learn how to study and yes that is true, but the reason is much deeper than that. Let me explain.

I have run into those in the cults many times in fact. I even have formal debates with them from time to time and the main thing that I find common among them is that they have taken Bible verses out of context and the sad thing is, they are getting people to fall for their lies because they do not know how to study the Bible for themselves. People hear someone that uses big words and sound like they know what they are talking about and the hook is set, they are falling for the lie and joining false churches. I know because I was almost one of them. Thank God I was raised in a Christian home and church, when I started to hear things that just did not sound right. I ran as fast as could from them.

One of the objections to learning how to interpret, is that people will say that the Bible is not left up to any private interpretation according to 2 Peter 1:20. Well, the fact is, they're right. We cannot use our own interpretation when it comes to studying the Bible. However, we all interpret when we read, we cannot help it. In fact, as you read this, you are interpreting right now. In other words, as you read something you think you are understanding the words you are reading. But, the question we have to ask ourselves; remember, earlier I said we need to ask questions and this is one of them and that is: is this what the Bible is really saying or is this what the Holy Spirit means? The fact, however, we all do this all the time even if we do not mean to.

We cannot come to the Bible with our own preconceived ideas and beliefs. What I mean by this is, we cannot come to the scriptures already believing that they teach a certain way. What I mean here is we cannot try to make the Bible say what we want it to because that is the way we believe.

Let me try and explain it with an example. Some people believe that the scriptures teach that we can lose our salvation, so they refuse to look at the scriptures in any other way. Of course the same can be said about those that believe in eternal security or once saved always saved.

So how do we overcome this? That is a good question and I am not sure I or anyone else can really answer this question however; if we could just let the scriptures speak for themselves then I think we could overcome this and not be afraid to let the scriptures correct what we believe.

What I mean by not being afraid to let the scriptures teach us is that we must have a teachable spirit. If we are not open to being taught or corrected, then we are being proud or prideful and look at what the Bible has to say about this.

1. 1Pe 5:5 "Likewise, ye younger, submit yourselves unto the elder. Yea, all *of you* be subject one to another, and be clothed with humility: for God

resisteth the proud, and giveth grace to the humble." (King James Version 1 Pet. 5:5)

2. Pro 13:18 "Poverty and shame *shall be to* him that refuseth instruction: but he that regardeth reproof shall be honoured." (King James Version Pro 13:18)
3. Prov. 12:1 "Anyone who loves learning accepts correction, but a person who hates being corrected is stupid." (New Century Version Prov. 12:1)
4. Prov. 15:32 "Those who refuse correction hate themselves, but those who accept correction gain understanding." (New Century Version Prov. 15:32)

So clearly we need to be teachable if not then why take the time to study. We need to be like David who said several times in Psalms Teach me oh Lord.

We can learn how to do it rightly just like the Bible says in 2Ti 2:15 "Study to shew thyself approved unto God, a workman that needeth not to be ashamed, rightly dividing the word of truth." (King James Version 2 Tim. 2:15)

Remember the Bible tells us in Isa 28:10 "For precept must be upon precept, precept upon precept; line upon line, line upon line; here a little, and there a little" (King James Version Isa 28:10). The way I like to put it is like this, you can look at like a jigsaw puzzle there are millions of pieces and if you put them together they make a beautiful picture. However if you get the pieces wrong or try to make them fit together when they don't you get something distorted. This is why we need to learn how to interpret the Bible so we get all the pieces put together right.

Yes we cannot interpret the Bible on our own that will lead us down a very bad path we do not want to be on however, the Bible will interpret itself and we have the Holy Spirit to teach us all things John 14:26 "But the Comforter, *which is* the Holy Ghost, whom the Father will send in my name, he shall teach you all things, and bring all things to your remembrance, whatsoever I have said unto you." (King James Version John 14:26)

You might or might not know this, but the Bibles we use every day are an interpretation. You might recall from chapter two that the original manuscripts were written in

Hebrew, Greek and Aramaic, so when the translators got together, they had to interpret what the originals were saying. Bibles such as the King James, New King James, Amplified, New American Standard, New Living Translation and more are just that translation or interpretation of the originals.

We also need to take into count that as much as we would like the Bible to be just plain in what it says, it just is not in many cases. We have to dig for the right interpretation. Look at the fact that even among Christian churches that not all plain text is so plain to others. For an example, I can read Rom 6:23 “For the wages of sin is death; but the gift of God is eternal life through Jesus Christ our Lord.” (King James Version Romans 6:23) and see eternal security where others see this verse as say we can lose our salvation. However, the other person and I are going to both say it is plainly there. So we need to learn to interpret the Bible if for no other reason so we can be sure of what we believe and why we believe and to know we are not out in left field somewhere.

So what we are going to learn in this chapter is something called Biblical hermeneutics which simply means the science of studying scripture.

There is a big word within hermeneutics (as if that is not big enough) and that is exegetical or exegesis which simply means the science of interpretation or the organized and logical study of the scriptures, so we can find out the original meaning of the text. Basically, what we are trying to do is interpret the scriptures in such a way that we that we might understand how the original readers or listeners would have heard it or read it. (Fee & Stuart, 2003, bottom of page 23)

Now, do not close the book and say I give up; this is not as hard as it sounds, we are not going to be mixing chemicals that can blow up or burn up the house with a bunsen burner lol, lol, it is not that kind of science, but we are going to learn the science of exegesis.

Actually, what exegesis does is gets into our hands the tools we need to accurately study the Bible and get the deep treasure out of it for our lives.

We must remember also that the Bible is written for both the spiritual man and the physical man. What I mean by this, is that there are spiritual applications and physical applications as well. I know you're probably thinking at this point I have lost my mind, trust me I lost that a long time ago lol, lol. Let me show you what I mean here; for the spiritual man we need salvation. Look at what Jesus told Nicodemus in John 3:5: "Jesus answered, Verily, verily, I say unto thee, Except a man be born of water and of the Spirit, he cannot enter into the kingdom of God." (King James Version John 3:5) Now for the physical Luke 6:31 "And as ye would that men should do to you, do ye also to them likewise." (King James Version Luke 6:31)

So we see that the Bible teaches us what we need to spiritually grow in Christ and how we are to live our life here on earth. Now, do not get me wrong here, I understand that the Bible is a spiritual book and everything in it helps us to grow closer to God. The point I am making here or trying to make here, is that there is both a spiritual application to the Bible such as spiritual warfare and a physical application such as a moral law.

So where do we go from here? Good question, I just hope you're not running around the room going goo goo, gaa gaa, over everything so far. Maybe this is a good place to just stop, put the book down, stretch, and get some fresh air before going on to the next chapter.

Chapter Questions

1 Because we have finite mind we can understand everything in the Bible? True or false
2. Cults take Bible verses out of what?
3. Can we use our own interpretation? Why or why not.
4. Can we let the scriptures speak for themselves? Why or why not.
5. Are we to be teachable? Who do you think are the teacher or teachers?
6. We need to learn to interpret the Bible if for no other reason so we can be sure of what?
7. The Bible is written for both the _______________ and the _______________
8. What is exegetical or exegesis?
9. The Bible teaches us what we need to spiritually grow in _____________
10. Why do you think two people can read the same passage of scripture and get two different interpretations?
11. Would being unsaved cause a person to interpret the Bible differently than someone saved? Why or why not.

References

Thomas Nelson, Inc, 2005, New Century Version, Retrieved November 17, 2012, from http://www.biblegateway.com

Fee G. & Stuart D., 2003, How to Read the Bible for All Its Worth, Publisher: Zondervan Grand Rapids MI.

Chapter Seven: Context, Context, Context

I think the major mistake I see people and cult groups do a lot is to take Bible verses out of context in more ways than one, so it this that we will deal with first. However, this is nothing new; the apostles had the same problem in their day as well. Look at 1 Peter 3:16-17 in the New Century Version it reads: "He writes about this in all his letters. Some things in Paul's letters are hard to understand, and people who are ignorant and weak in faith explain these things falsely. They also falsely explain the other Scriptures, but they are destroying themselves by doing this. Dear friends, since you already know about this, be very careful. Do not let those evil people lead you away by the wrong they do. Be careful so you will not fall from your strong faith." New Century Version 2 Peter 3:16-17)

The Word of God has spoken to every generation from the time of Adam and Eve to Paul and Peter and to us this very day and time. It is our job as biblical interpreters not to explain the Bible so much as it is to gain clarification or understanding so that we can apply the Word to our lives and proclaim the good news in such a way that others can understand it and come into the great relationship with the Triune God as we do. So where do we go from here? Context, context, and more context.

When we think of context what we mean is don't make the verse say something it does not. An example: if my wife comes out in a new dress and asks me how it looks and I respond with honey, I don't like the dress on you, she might respond with, oh sure, you don't think I look good. No dear, that is not what I said (She took what I said out of context). What I said was, the dress does not look good on you. Let's see now how people do this with Bible. Here is a Bible example: 2Co 6:14 "Be ye not unequally yoked together with unbelievers: for what fellowship hath righteousness with unrighteousness? And what communion hath light with darkness?" (King James Version 2 Cor. 6:14) People, for whatever their reasons, try to use this verse to say that people of different races should not marry. However, that is not what that verse says at all, what it does say however, is we are not to marry those that believe differently than we do or to be married to an unsaved person.

Simply put, do not make the meaning of the words something they are not and do not take them out of context with the topic in which they are used or take them out of context with the verses surrounding it. I have often told people who ask me, what does this verse mean, to look to the verses before and after and sometimes read the whole chapter and in some cases read the whole book. Most of the time, the immediate answer is found within the texts itself.

To keep things in the proper context, we must ask why the writer is writing what he wrote. We need to figure out what their train of thought was because most of the time as we talk we finish our train of thought before we move on to another topic (I say most of the time, because that rule does not always apply, especially in the Bible).

One of the problems I have seen time and time again, is that people get things out of context because the King James and others break the Bible up into single verses and not into paragraphs or into topic groups. Let me show you what I mean here. We will use the book of Jude simply because it is a short book.

King James Version Jude

Jude 1:1 Jude, the servant of Jesus Christ, and brother of James, to them that are sanctified by God the Father, and preserved in Jesus Christ, *and* called:
Jude 1:2 Mercy unto you, and peace, and love, be multiplied.
Jude 1:3 Beloved, when I gave all diligence to write unto you of the common salvation, it was needful for me to write unto you, and exhort *you* that ye should earnestly contend for the faith which was once delivered unto the saints.
Jude 1:4 For there are certain men crept in unawares, who were before of old ordained to this condemnation, ungodly men, turning the grace of our God into lasciviousness, and denying the only Lord God, and our Lord Jesus Christ.
Jude 1:5 I will therefore put you in remembrance, though ye once knew this, how that the Lord, having saved the people

out of the land of Egypt, afterward destroyed them that believed not.
Jude 1:6 And the angels which kept not their first estate, but left their own habitation, he hath reserved in everlasting chains under darkness unto the judgment of the great day.
Jude 1:7 Even as Sodom and Gomorrha, and the cities about them in like manner, giving themselves over to fornication, and going after strange flesh, are set forth for an example, suffering the vengeance of eternal fire.
Jude 1:8 Likewise also these *filthy* dreamers defile the flesh, despise dominion, and speak evil of dignities.
Jude 1:9 Yet Michael the archangel, when contending with the devil he disputed about the body of Moses, durst not bring against him a railing accusation, but said, The Lord rebuke thee.
Jude 1:10 But these speak evil of those things which they know not: but what they know naturally, as brute beasts, in those things they corrupt themselves.
Jude 1:11 Woe unto them! for they have gone in the way of Cain, and ran greedily after the error of Balaam for reward, and perished in the gainsaying of Core.
Jude 1:12 These are spots in your feasts of charity, when they feast with you, feeding themselves without fear: clouds *they are* without water, carried about of winds; trees whose fruit withereth, without fruit, twice dead, plucked up by the roots;
Jude 1:13 Raging waves of the sea, foaming out their own shame; wandering stars, to whom is reserved the blackness of darkness for ever.
Jude 1:14 And Enoch also, the seventh from Adam, prophesied of these, saying, Behold, the Lord cometh with ten thousands of his saints,
Jude 1:15 To execute judgment upon all, and to convince all that are ungodly among them of all their ungodly deeds which they have ungodly committed, and of all their hard *speeches* which ungodly sinners have spoken against him.
Jude 1:16 These are murmurers, complainers, walking after their own lusts; and their mouth speaketh great swelling

words, having men's persons in admiration because of advantage.
Jude 1:17 But, beloved, remember ye the words which were spoken before of the apostles of our Lord Jesus Christ;
Jude 1:18 How that they told you there should be mockers in the last time, who should walk after their own ungodly lusts.
Jude 1:19 These be they who separate themselves, sensual, having not the Spirit.
Jude 1:20 But ye, beloved, building up yourselves on your most holy faith, praying in the Holy Ghost,
Jude 1:21 Keep yourselves in the love of God, looking for the mercy of our Lord Jesus Christ unto eternal life.
Jude 1:22 And of some have compassion, making a difference:
Jude 1:23 And others save with fear, pulling *them* out of the fire; hating even the garment spotted by the flesh.
Jude 1:24 Now unto him that is able to keep you from falling, and to present *you* faultless before the presence of his glory with exceeding joy,
Jude 1:25 To the only wise God our Saviour, *be* glory and majesty, dominion and power, both now and ever. Amen.

The temptation here is to single out a verse from the rest of the text, this is what gets us to take verses out of context. So now let's see how the first century reader would see this same book.

King James Version Jude

Jude, the servant of Jesus Christ, and brother of James, to them that are sanctified by God the Father, and preserved in Jesus Christ, *and* called: Mercy unto you, and peace, and love, be multiplied.

Beloved, when I gave all diligence to write unto you of the common salvation, it was needful for me to write unto you, and exhort *you* that ye should earnestly contend for the faith which was once delivered unto the saints. For there are certain men crept in unawares, who were before of old ordained to this condemnation, ungodly men, turning the grace of our God into lasciviousness, and denying the only Lord God, and our Lord Jesus Christ. I will therefore put you in remembrance, though ye once knew this, how that the

Lord, having saved the people out of the land of Egypt, afterward destroyed them that believed not. And the angels which kept not their first estate, but left their own habitation, he hath reserved in everlasting chains under darkness unto the judgment of the great day. Even as Sodom and Gomorrha, and the cities about them in like manner, giving themselves over to fornication, and going after strange flesh, are set forth for an example, suffering the vengeance of eternal fire. Likewise also these *filthy* dreamers defile the flesh, despise dominion, and speak evil of dignities. Yet Michael the archangel, when contending with the devil he disputed about the body of Moses, durst not bring against him a railing accusation, but said, The Lord rebuke thee. But these speak evil of those things which they know not: but what they know naturally, as brute beasts, in those things they corrupt themselves. Woe unto them! for they have gone in the way of Cain, and ran greedily after the error of Balaam for reward, and perished in the gainsaying of Core. These are spots in your feasts of charity, when they feast with you, feeding themselves without fear: clouds they are without water, carried about of winds; trees whose fruit withereth, without fruit, twice dead, plucked up by the roots; Raging waves of the sea, foaming out their own shame; wandering stars, to whom is reserved the blackness of darkness for ever. And Enoch also, the seventh from Adam, prophesied of these, saying, Behold, the Lord cometh with ten thousands of his saints, To execute judgment upon all, and to convince all that are ungodly among them of all their ungodly deeds which they have ungodly committed, and of all their hard speeches which ungodly sinners have spoken against him. These are murmurers, complainers, walking after their own lusts; and their mouth speaketh great swelling words, having men's persons in admiration because of advantage.

But, beloved, remember ye the words which were spoken before of the apostles of our Lord Jesus Christ; How that they told you there should be mockers in the last time, who should walk after their own ungodly lusts. These be they who separate themselves, sensual, having not the Spirit. But ye, beloved, building up yourselves on your most holy faith, praying in the Holy Ghost, Keep yourselves in the love of God, looking for the mercy of our Lord Jesus Christ unto eternal life. And of some have compassion, making a difference: And others save with fear, pulling them out of the fire; hating even the garment spotted by the flesh.

Now unto him that is able to keep you from falling, and to present *you* faultless before the presence of his glory with exceeding joy, To the only wise God our Saviour, *be* glory and majesty, dominion and power, both now and ever. Amen.

Now it is a lot easier to keep everything in its proper context. I suggest you do this: find the beginning of the paragraph and put the whole paragraph together. Another thing you can do is title each paragraph; here, let me show you with Jude again.

Salutations or Greetings

Jude, the servant of Jesus Christ, and brother of James, to them that are sanctified by God the Father, and preserved in Jesus Christ, *and* called: Mercy unto you, and peace, and love, be multiplied.

Beloved, when I gave all diligence to write unto you of the common salvation, it was needful for me to write unto you, and exhort *you* that ye should earnestly contend for the faith which was once delivered unto the saints. For there are certain men crept in unawares, who were before of old ordained to this condemnation, ungodly men, turning the grace of our God into lasciviousness, and denying the only Lord God, and our Lord Jesus Christ. I will therefore put you in remembrance, though ye once knew this, how that the Lord, having saved the people out of the land of Egypt, afterward destroyed them that believed not. And the angels which kept not their first estate, but left their own habitation, he hath reserved in everlasting chains under darkness unto the judgment of the great day. Even as Sodom and Gomorrha, and the cities about them in like manner, giving themselves over to fornication, and going after strange flesh, are set forth for an example, suffering the vengeance of eternal fire. Likewise also these *filthy* dreamers defile the flesh, despise dominion, and speak evil of dignities. Yet Michael the archangel, when contending with the devil he disputed about the body of Moses, durst not bring against him a railing accusation, but said, The Lord rebuke thee. But these speak evil of those things which they know not: but what they know naturally, as brute beasts, in those things they corrupt themselves. Woe unto them! for they have gone in the way of Cain, and ran greedily after the error of Balaam for reward, and perished in the gainsaying of Core. These are spots in your feasts of charity, when they feast with you, feeding themselves without fear: clouds they are without water, carried about of winds; trees whose fruit withereth, without fruit, twice dead, plucked up by the roots; Raging waves of the sea, foaming out their own shame; wandering stars, to whom is reserved the blackness of darkness for ever. And Enoch also, the seventh from Adam, prophesied of these, saying, Behold, the Lord cometh with ten thousands of his saints, To execute judgment upon all, and to convince all that are ungodly among them of all their ungodly deeds which they have ungodly committed, and of all their hard speeches which ungodly sinners have spoken against him. These are murmurers, complainers, walking after their own lusts; and their mouth speaketh great swelling words, having men's persons in admiration because of advantage.

I think you get the point here. However, by doing little things like this will help us to keep everything straight or in its proper context.

To put in an interesting note here, the Bible was not written into chapters and verses like we have today therefore we need to be careful and remember the chapters and verses are simply there to help us find things faster. "The chapter divisions commonly used today was developed by Stephen Langton, an Archbishop of Canterbury. Langton put the modern chapter divisions into place in around A.D. 1227. The Wycliffe English Bible of 1382 was the first Bible to use this chapter pattern. Since the Wycliffe Bible, nearly all Bible translations have followed Langton's chapter divisions.

The Hebrew Old Testament was divided into verses by a Jewish rabbi by the name of Nathan in A.D. 1448. Robert Estienne, who was also known as Stephanus, was the first to divide the New Testament into standard numbered verses, in 1555. Stephanus essentially used Nathan's verse divisions for the Old Testament. Since that time, beginning with the Geneva Bible, the chapter and verse divisions employed by Stephanus have been accepted into nearly all the Bible versions." (Who divided the Bible into chapters and verses? Why and when was it done? (2012, para. 2 & 3)

Another way we can keep things in its proper context is by understanding how we read. According to Mortimer J. Adler, Charles Van Doren in their book "How to Read a Book" (1972, pp. 17, 18, 19 & 29) there are four levels of reading and they are:

1. Rudimentary or basic and we learn it in elementary school and at this level we are simply reading no deep interpretation just understanding the basic meaning of the words. When we learnt to read the basic simple sentence as see Jain run, in this we don't care why Jain is running we are just trying to understand the meaning of the words and are happy we can read.
2. Inspectional reading, this is usually when a reader does not have a lot of time, so they quickly skim over the book to get a general idea of the story. The question that this reader will be able to answer or should be able to answer is what the book is about. The reader should also be able to answer what Genre it falls into.
3. Analytical reading the reader in this case studies the book in-depth analyzing it looking up words to find the meaning. The reader is looking at everything in order get the clearest understanding of what was written. I look at this as almost doing a jigsaw puzzle they are looking at the pieces to fit them together to get the big picture. In other words the reader is trying to understand its message as completely as possible. I suppose the other way you can look at this

it is like looking at painting studding every fine detail to try and figure out the message behind the painting.

4. Syntopical reading simply put the reader takes the message and compares it with other books that go along with or are of the same related text for the purpose of building a detailed understanding of the text and trying to get to the original meaning of the text.

The thing here is that all levels are dependent upon each other. Simply put, you have to have all 4 in order to basically be able to go beyond the Rudimentary or basic level.

Now do not get too worked up over this, I put this in here so you are aware of how we read. By understanding how we do things then we can do them better.

The thing that I wanted to mention here is when you do the skimming or just reading don't not get concerned about details. Remember, you're just getting the general idea of the book or chapter or paragraph you are studying. A good tip is, just take quick notes as you read, this will also help you to stay focused and keep your mind from wandering and give you notes for later on when you study other things. Remember, the purpose of interpretation is to get the basic meaning of the text. All of this will help us to keep things in its proper context.

Now the thing about context is that we need to look to the experts from time to time I mean let's face not all of us our history buffs. However we need to be careful because there are sources out there that are not Christian friendly. However, we can use recourses like the internet, documentaries, libraries, Bible dictionaries and of course your pastor and the Bible teachers of church that is one of the reasons they are there and that is to help you get the most out of your Bible studies.

While we are talking about getting outside help, there are two other sources or tools every student of the bible should have. They are Matthew Henry's concise commentary on the whole Bible and Strong's concordance. Now the nice thing about these two things is if you have a computer you can get both for free from e-sword.net, the nice thing about this program is you get the King James Bible with and without the Strong's numbers and you can get more commentaries and Bibles and Bible dictionaries along with a lot of other things now there are some stuff that you have to pay for, but most of it is free. I use the program all time in fact I would be lost without it I am getting a table so I can have e-sword on the go.

I cannot stress this enough I think the most important tool next to the Holy Spirit is the Strong's concordance due to the fact that we need to understand the definition of words. Now I know your thinking because I thought the same thing I know what words mean however, the words in the Bible do not always mean what we think they do. We must remember the King James Version was written in 1611 the meaning of words change over time, Not only, but from one culture to another the meaning of words change, a word that is a complement in one culture could be an insult in another.

Let me show you what I am talking about here because we must understand that the words in the Bible do now always mean what we think. In fact the same word can have two different meanings in the same verse. So for this example we are going to look at Romans 5:20 it says: Rom 5:20 "Moreover the law entered, that the offence might abound. But where sin abounded, grace did much more abound" (King James Version Rom. 5:20)

Now the two words we are going to look at here are abound. In the first part of the verse we see "Moreover the law entered, that the offence might abound." So let's look at the meaning of the word abounded here, it means: "pleh-on-ad'-zo to do, make or be more, that is, increase (transitively or intransitively); by extension to superabound: - abound, abundant, make to increase, have over." So we can read the first part of that verse this way: "Moreover the law entered, that the offence might increase.

Now the last part of that verse says: "grace did much more abound" Now let's see the meaning of the word abound again it means: "hoop-er-per-is-syoo'-o to super abound: - abound much more, exceeding." So it can be read this way: "grace did much abound much more"

So we can see here that Paul was saying even if sin may increase that Gods grace will about even much more. So we can clearly see here how the same word can have different meanings. So it is important to know the meaning of the words so we can keep things in its proper context.

Now just as important as knowing the meaning of the words is content. Now content simply means letting the passage say what it means not what we want it to mean as I have said before.

We must also understand grammatical relationships within the text. The changing of words or the meaning of words can change the whole meaning of the text. Here is a great example of this. In the Jehovah's Witnesses Bible in John 1:1 it reads "In the beginning was the word and the word was with God and the word was a god." (New World Translation John 1:1) Now the King James Version says: John 1:1 "In the beginning was the Word, and the Word was with God, and the Word was God. (King James Version John 1:1) Now at first glance you would think they are saying the same thing however, if you look at the New World Translation they add a little letter "a" look at it again reads "In the beginning was the word and the word was with God and the word was a god." (New World Translation John 1:1) Now by adding this little letter they have changed the whole meaning of the text and who Jesus is. What they done here is totally done away with the trinity by making Jesus a God now what we have is two gods not one.

So we can see here how the words are used in a sentence makes a big difference in our understanding of the scriptures.

The other thing I would like to point out is watch for punctuations. If we miss something like a comma we could miss the whole meaning of the topic and or verse. Let me show you what I am talking about. Before I get started here I want to point out that I am not saying one translation is better than the other, I will leave that up to you however this is just an example.

In Ephesians 4:11-12 Paul says this: "And he gave some, apostles; and some, prophets; and some, evangelists;

and some, pastors and teachers; For the perfecting of the saints, for the work of the ministry, for the edifying of the body of Christ:" If we were to look at these verse we would see that there is a comma after each the duties of the five fold ministry. Now with that in mind we see that those duties are three things "For the perfecting of the saints, for the work of the ministry, for the edifying of the body of Christ:" (King James Version Eph 4:11-12) however, if we were to look at another translation we would see that they leave out the commas. "For the training of the saints as servants in the church, for the building up of the body of Christ" (Bible In Basic English Eph. 4:12) As we see here this version leaves out the commas and only list two duties the fivefold ministry. So what I am trying to get at here is if we miss the punctuations we might miss something important.

Now let's take a look at this from another point. Not only is punctuations important, but sentence structure is just as important. What I mean by this is we need to understand how sentences work. For example the semicolon is used when you need to join two complete sentences together for an example It was the best of times; it was the worst of times. Dickens could wrote that this way It was the best of times. It was the worst of times. Or he could have done it this way It was the best of times, and it was the worst of times. The semicolon is also used when the two shorter sentences are closely related like this Life is just to hard; to dang hard to keep going.

So how does this relate to the Bible well let's take a look at a verse here "For the wages of sin is death; but the gift of God is eternal life through Jesus Christ our Lord." (King James Version Rom. 6:23) Now there are some that will say that this verse shows we can lose our salvation however, they fail to understand sentences structure. Now the first part of this verse clearly says that the wages or the payment of sin is death, but the thing is if we look at the structure we would see a semicolon followed by a, but therefore canceling out the first part of verse. Now because of that the rest of the verse is in affect "but the gift of God is eternal life through Jesus Christ our Lord" Now that the first part of the verse is canceled we are left with eternal salvation, therefore we cannot lose it. Now if we miss the semicolon and the, but or we miss the sentences structure we will miss what great news God is trying to tells.

Chapter Questions

1. When we take things out of context we risk of making the verse say something ______________________

2. To keep things in the proper context, we must ask what?

3. Was the original manuscripts written in chapter and verses like we have today?

4. Another way we can keep things in its proper context is by understanding how we ______________

5. Would agree or disagree with this statement. How most people approach and read the Bible is through rudimentary reading? Why or why not?

6. Is it ok to just read to get a general idea of the book or chapter? Why or why not?

7. A good tip is, just take quick notes as you read. True or false

8. The changing of words or the meaning of words can what?

9. Is understanding sentence structure important why or why not?

10. Give an example of sentence structure.

References

Adler M., Van Doren C., 1972, How to Read a Book, Revised and updated, published by, New York: Simon and Schuster, NY NY.

Got question, 2011, Who divided the Bible into chapters and verses? Why and when was it done?, 2012, Retrieved November 28, 2012, from http://www.gotquestions.org/divided-Bible-chapters-verses.

Chapter Eight Putting it Together

Study thesis: With in this study we are going to be looking at salvation, more to the point I am going to prove why we need to be saved, is salvation right away or is it in the future and finally the fact that we are eternally secured.

Why we need to be saved

1. Rom. 3:23 "For all have sinned, and come short of the glory of God"
    a. The word all is really self explanatory however, for sake of argument we will look at this word in the Greek and it means: *pas* Including all the forms of declension; apparently a primary word; *all*, *any*, *every*, the *whole:* - all (manner of, means) alway (-s), any (one), X daily, + ever, every (one, way), as many as, + no (-thing), X throughly, whatsoever, whole, whosoever.
2. What does this mean for me?
    a. So here we can clearly see that all literally means everyone including me.
3. How could this apply to me?
    a. In Gen. 2:16-17 God told Adam and Eve not to eat of the tree of knowledge of good and evil. They did eat it, but they did not die physically why?
4. Physical Death
    a. What I am about to say here might seem like it goes against the normal teaching on this, but hang in there with me.
    b. First let me start by saying that some verses have more than one meaning and this verse is no exception.

c. In Gen. 2:17 we see God tell Adam and Eve they will "surely die". I have to admit this is a little odd however, surely and die in the Hebrew is the same word with the same meaning. *Mooth* A primitive root; to *die* (literally or figuratively); causatively to *kill:* - X at all, X crying, (be) dead (body, man, one), (put to, worthy of) death, destroy (-er), (cause to, be like to, must) die, kill, necro [-mancer], X must needs, slay, X surely, X very suddenly, X in [no] wise.

d. We have to ask ourseleves the question did they die? The answer is yes the did and no not right away.
e. Let us deal with the not right away part first. Understanding sentence structure and how words were used back then is verry imoortant.
f. First off they in the first century church would have that part of the verse this way "dying, die" Now they would have had no problem understing however, for us it is a little difficult do to the fact we dont use the same word twice because there is no changed emphasis when a word is repeated.
g. What this means and what they knew it meant is that the day they eat it was their death sentence would start or that they would start to die. If God ment that they would die instently He would have only used the word die once.
h. The word day is kind of misleading as well because we assume that it ment that day they would die

however, the word day here does not mean a litteral 24day like we think so what does it mean then? Good question and if you rember I said in a earlyer chapter we must let the Bible interprit it self and this is what we need to do here.

i. 1 Ki 2:37 "For it shall be, that on the day thou goest out, and passest over the brook Kidron, thou shalt know for certain that thou shalt surely die: thy blood shall be upon thine own head." Now this is the same day as used in Gen. 2:17.

j. Just as in Gen. 2:17 this day is refurning to an action not a litteral day. "This verse uses yom (day) and the dual muwth just as Genesis 2:17 did. In Genesis 2:17, yom referred to the action (eating) in the same way that yom refers to the action here (go out and cross over). In neither case do they mean that was the particular day that death would come, but the particular day they did what they weren't supposed to do." (Hodge, 2010, section What is Yom Reerring to para 2) So simply put the word day is referring to the action of eating or crossing over and the moment they did that tnere days were going to be limited and evenchually die.

k. We know that Adam and Eve did die 900+ Years latter. This is why Paul could write Rom 6:23 "For the wages of sin is death; but the gift of God is eternal life through Jesus Christ our Lord." (King James Version Rom.

6:23) Sin or more to the point because of Adam's and Eve's sin physicall death entered into the world and therefore the moment we are born we are starting to die.

5. Spiritual death
    a. If we look at what happened because they did eat of the forbidden fruit we see that God cast them out of the garden Gen. 3:22-23.
    b. I hear the question, but God only did that so they would not live forever right? Yes however, we also see that they no longer could walk with God like they did in the Garden. Simply put they were separated from God's presence. Simply put they were separated from God. This is true spiritual death.
    c. Also if we look at Gen. 3:8 that when Adam and Eve heard God in the garden they hid themselves from God, but look at the next verse it says God called out to Adam and asked him where he was. "Then they heard the LORD God walking in the garden during the cool part of the day, and the man and his wife hid from the LORD God among the trees in the garden. But the LORD God called to the man and said, "Where are you?" (New Century Version Gen. 3:8-9)
    d. Did God know where they were? Yes He knows everything, but when God asked "where are you" it shows that the close fellowship they had with each other was gone, it was indeed broken.

e. In Eph. 4:18 Paul tells us that we where "alienated from the life of God" being alienated is the same as being separated from and being separated from God is the same as not having life, for only in God do we have life.
f. In Eph. 2:1 we read "And you [*hath he quickened*], who were dead in trespasses and sins;" (King James Version Eph. 2:1) We can clearly see here that before salvation we were indeed dead.
    i. Now we are all physically alive so this must mean spiritually dead.
g. This gets backed up even more in Col. 2:13 "And you, being dead in your sins and the uncircumcision of your flesh, hath he quickened together with him, having forgiven you all trespasses." (King James Version Col. 2:13)
h. So clearly we can see we are born separated from God and that is spiritual death.

6. Is salvation right away or is it in the future?
    a. In Romans 8:30 we read "Moreover whom he did predestinate, them he also called: and whom he called, them he also justified: and whom he justified, them he also glorified." (King James Version Rom. 8:30)
        i. The key words here are justified and glorified. These words show us that we are indeed made right with God now not in the future.

b. Also in Romans 8:33-34 we read "Who shall lay any thing to the charge of God's elect? [*It is*] God that justifieth. Who [*is*] he that condemneth? [*It is*] Christ that died, yea rather, that is risen again, who is even at the right hand of God, who also maketh intercession for us." (King James Version Rom. 8:33-34)
    i. Here we can plainly see that we are justified and not condemned.
c. In Titus 3:5 we read "Not by works of righteousness which we have done, but according to his mercy he saved us, by the washing of regeneration, and renewing of the Holy Ghost;" (King James Version Titus 3:5)
    i. Clearly this verse says we are saved not we are going to be saved.
d. In John 3:15 we see "That whosoever believeth in him should not perish, but have eternal life."
    i. We see here if we believe we have eternal life. The word have is a present tense word not future.
e. In John 3:18 we read "He that believeth on him is not condemned: but he that believeth not is condemned already, because he hath not believed in the name of the only begotten Son of God." (King James Version John 3:18)
    i. Here we see if we believe we are not condemned, but those

that believe not are already condemned.

7. In John 5:24 Jesus says "Verily, verily, I say unto you, He that heareth my word, and believeth on him that sent me, hath everlasting life, and shall not come into condemnation; but is passed from death unto life."
    a. The word hath means "verb (used with object), present singular 1st person have, 2nd have or (Archaic) hast, 3rd has or (Archaic) hath, present plural have; past singular 1st person had, 2nd had or (Archaic) hadst or haddest, 3rd had, past plural had; past participle had; present participle having. 1.to possess; own; hold for use; contain:" http://dictionary.reference.com/browse/hath)
        i. So we see here that hath is a present tense word and Jesus said "if we believe in Him we have eternal life."
        ii. If Jesus meant in the future he would have use something like will have, but He did not he said we have it now.
    b. Look at 1 John 5:11-13 that says "And this is the record, that God hath given to us eternal life, and this life is in his Son. He that hath the Son hath life; [*and*] he that hath not the Son of God hath not life. These things have I written unto you that

believe on the name of the Son of God; that ye may know that ye have eternal life, and that ye may believe on the name of the Son of God." (King James Version 1 John 5:11-13)

i. I think it is clear when John says that "ye may know that ye have eternal life" we never have to question our salvation or hope for our salvation we can rest in the fact that we now have eternal life.

8. Are we eternally secured or can we lose our salvation?

a. With trying sound redundant here most of the Bible verses we have looked at so far on salvation uses the term eternal. We also saw that we have salvation now or eternal life now.

b. If one could lose their salvation then it could not be eternal it would have to be temporary.

i. Now let's look at Rom. 6:23 it says: "For the wages of sin [is] death; but the gift of God [is] eternal life through Jesus Christ our Lord." (King James Version Rom. 6:23)

ii. I know I used this verse before to show sentence structure however, it shows that we are eternally secure in and only in Christ Jesus.

c. Let's look at Eph. 1:13-14 it says "In whom ye also [*trusted*], after that ye heard the word of truth, the gospel of your salvation: in whom also after that ye believed, ye were sealed with that holy Spirit of promise, Which is the earnest of our inheritance until the redemption of the purchased possession, unto the praise of his glory. " (King James Version Eph. 1:13-14)

i. The words I want us to look at here are earnest and inheritance.
ii. "earnest" means a pledge or a down payment. the Holy Spirit is given to the believer as a pledge or a down payment that they will finally receive eternal life. And our inheritance is Heaven.

d. In 2 Corth. 5:17 it says: "herefore if any man [*be*] in Christ, [*he is*] a new creature: old things are passed away; behold, all things are become new" (King James Version 2 Corth. 5:17)

i. It says we are a new creature in order for us to lose our salvation we have to be changed back and God is not going to do that to His children.

e. In 1 Pet. 1:18-19 we see that we have been redeemed by the blood of Jesus. "Forasmuch as ye know that ye were not redeemed with corruptible things, [*as*] silver and gold, from your vain conversation [*received*] by tradition from your fathers; But with the precious blood of Christ, as of a lamb without blemish and without spot:" (King James Version 1 Pet. 1:18-19)

            i. The word redeemed means to pay with a price and that was done by Jesus dyeing on the cross.
                1. If we could lose our salvation that God would have to take back Christ or revoke his payment. God is not going to do that after all look at the high price he paid.

f. In Jude 1:24 we read: "Now unto him that is able to keep you from falling, and to present [*you*] faultless before the presence of his glory with exceeding joy" (King James Version Jude 1:24)
    i. Here we have to ask ourselves, does God lie? The answer is no He does not. Here we see we are promised he will keep us from falling.
g. The Bible also teaches us that we are preserved in 2 Tim. 4:18"And the Lord shall deliver me from every evil work, and will preserve [*me*] unto his heavenly kingdom: to whom [*be*] glory for ever and ever. Amen. And in Jude, "Jude, the servant of Jesus Christ, and brother of James, to them that are sanctified by God the Father, and preserved in Jesus Christ, [*and*] called: Mercy unto you, and peace, and love, be multiplied." (King

James Version 2 Tim. 4:18 and Jude 1:1)

  i. In these two verses we see that we are preserved. Now preserved in the Greek means "G5083 G5083 to 1. guard (from loss or injury) 2. *(properly)* by keeping the eye upon, i.e. to note (a prophecy) 3. *(... figuratively)* to fulfil a command 4. *(by implication)* to detain in custody 5. *(... figuratively)* to maintain 6. *(by extension)* to withhold for personal ends 7. *(... figuratively)* to keep unmarried (Meyers, E-Sword (Version 10.1 Computer Software 2012, Strong's dictionary)
  ii. Clearly from the word preserved we can see we are truly secure.

h. It never seems to fail when talking about eternal security someone will say but you can walk away from God. Is this true?
  i. First off if we were to look at the vast amount of examples of men who have sinned we see people like David who slept with another man's wife and got her pregnant and had her husband killed, but yet did not lose his salvation. Moses sinned and was not allowed into the promises land, but yet did not lose his salvation. There

are many more that sinned however; they did not lose their salvation.

ii. We must also remember that God will not forsake his children, Hebrews 13:5, Ps. 94:14. We can backslide, but He is right there with us.

iii. Also we must remember that God does not believe in divorce and the Bible tells us that He married to the backslider, Jer. 3:14

i. What about the Bible verse in 1 Tim. 4:1 that says: "Now the Spirit speaketh expressly, that in the latter times some shall depart from the faith, giving heed to seducing spirits, and doctrines of devils" (King James Version 1 Tim.4:1)

   i. It does say that some will depart from the faith, but does this mean they were of the faith? Just because someone goes to church faithfully or takes part in church activities does not make them in the faith just a part of it.

   ii. 1 John 2:19 "They went out from us, but they were not of us; for if they had been of us, they would [*no doubt*] have continued with us: but [*they went out*], that they might be made manifest that they were not all of us."

   iii. John clearly teaches us that if one truly departs from the faith they were never in the faith to begin with that is they were never saved

j. So how do we know if we are truly saved?
    i. It is clear in scripture that if we are saved we will have the works to back it up.
    ii. James 2:17 “Even so faith, if it hath not works, is dead, being alone.” (King James Version James 2:17)

I think it safe to say that this study could go on forever however, if I keep going this book will never get done.

As you can see from this chapter that if we take the time to study and dig into the word we find some really great things or hidden treasure that is better than silver and gold.

It is my prayer that this little book, even though it does not cover everything on the topic, that it at least inspires you to get into the Bible.

References

hath. (n.d.). *The Dictionary of American Slang*. Retrieved September 21, 2014, from Dictionary.com website: http://dictionary.reference.com/browse/hath

Meyers M., 2012, preserved, E-Sword, Version 10.1 Computer Software, Strong's dictionary, Retrieved September 21/2014

www.ingramcontent.com/pod-product-compliance
Ingram Content Group UK Ltd.
Pitfield, Milton Keynes, MK11 3LW, UK
UKHW041939190726
13854UKWH00004B/1685